MTTC 96

Basic Skills

Teacher Certification Exam

By: Sharon Wynne, M.S
Southern Connecticut State University

"And, while there's no reason yet to panic, I think it's only prudent that we make preparations to panic."

XAMonline, INC.
Boston

To obtain permission(s) to use the material from this work for any purpose including workshops or seminars, please submit a written request to:

XAMonline, Inc.
21 Orient Ave.
Melrose, MA 02176
Toll Free 1-800-301-4647
Email: winwin1111@aol.com
Web www.xamonline.com
Fax: 1-718-662-9268

Library of Congress Cataloging-in-Publication Data

Wynne, Sharon A.
  MTTC: Basic Skills 96   Teacher Certification / Sharon A. Wynne.
  ISBN: 978-1-58197-968-8
  1. MTTC: Basic Skills 96   2. Study Guides.   3. MTTC
  4. Teachers' Certification & Licensure.   5. Careers

Disclaimer:
The opinions expressed in this publication are the sole works of XAMonline and were created independently from the National Education Association, Educational Testing Service, or any State Department of Education, National Evaluation Systems or other testing affiliates.

Between the time of publication and printing, state specific standards as well as testing formats and website information may change that is not included in part or in whole within this product. Sample test questions are developed by XAMonline and reflect similar content as on real tests; however, they are not former tests. XAMonline assembles content that aligns with state standards but makes no claims nor guarantees teacher candidates a passing score. Numerical scores are determined by testing companies such as NES or ETS and then are compared with individual state standards. A passing score varies from state to state.

Printed in the United States of America

MTTC: Basic Skills
ISBN: 978-1-58197-968-8

Table of Contents

DOMAIN I.   **READING**

COMPETENCY 1.0 DETERMINE THE MEANING OF WORDS AND PHRASES 1

Skill 1.1   *Use the context of a passage to determine the meaning of words with multiple meanings, unfamiliar and uncommon words and phrases, and figurative expressions* 1

COMPETENCY 2.0 UNDERSTAND THE MAIN IDEA AND SUPPORTING DETAILS IN WRITTEN MATERIAL. 5

Skill 2.1   *Identify explicit and implicit main ideas.* 5

Skill 2.2   *Recognize ideas that support, illustrate, or elaborate the main idea of a passage* 6

COMPETENCY 3.0 IDENTIFY A WRITER'S PURPOSE, POINT OF VIEW, AND INTENDED MEANING 8

Skill 3.1   *Recognize a writer's expressed or implied purpose for writing.* 8

Skill 3.2   *Evaluate the appropriateness of written material for various purposes or audiences.* 9

Skill 3.3   *Recognize the likely effect of a writer's choice of words on an audience.* 10

Skill 3.4   *Use the content, word choice, and phrasing of a passage to determine a writer's opinion or point of view.* 10

COMPETENCY 4.0 ANALYZE THE RELATIONSHIP AMONG IDEAS IN WRITTEN MATERIAL 12

Skill 4.1   *Identify the sequence of events or steps* 12

Skill 4.2   *Identify cause-effect relationships* 12

Skill 4.3   *Analyze relationships between ideas in opposition.* 13

Skill 4.4   *Identify solutions to problems.* 15

Skill 4.5   *Draw conclusions inductively and deductively from information stated or implied in a passage.* 15

COMPETENCY 5.0 USE CRITICAL REASONING SKILLS TO EVALUATE WRITTEN MATERIAL 18

Skill 5.1   Evaluate the stated or implied assumptions on which the validity of a writer's argument depends. 18

Skill 5.2   Judge the relevance or importance of facts, examples, or graphic data to a writer's argument. 19

Skill 5.3   Evaluate the logic of a writer's argument. 19

Skill 5.4   Evaluate the validity of analogies. 21

Skill 5.5   Distinguish between fact and opinion. 22

Skill 5.6   Assess the credibility or objectivity of the writer or source of written material. 23

COMPETENCY 6.0 APPLY STUDY SKILLS TO READING ASSIGNMENTS 26

Skill 6.1   Organize and summarize information for study purposes. 26

Skill 6.2   Follow written instructions or directions. 27

Skill 6.3   Interpret information presented in charts, graphs, or tables. 28

Sample Test: Reading 31

Answer Key 39

Answers with Rationale 40

DOMAIN II.   MATHEMATICS

COMPETENCY 7.0 USE NUMBER CONCEPTS AND COMPUTATION SKILLS **44**

Skill 7.1   Add, subtract, multiply, divide fractions, decimals, and integers........ 44

Skill 7.2   Use the order of operations to solve problems. 58

Skill 7.3   Solve problems involving percents. 59

Skill 7.4   Perform calculations using exponents and scientific notation............ 60

Skill 7.5   Estimate solutions to problems... 62

Skill 7.6   Use the concepts of "less than" and "greater than." 64

COMPETENCY 8.0 SOLVE WORD PROBLEMS INVOLVING INTEGERS, FRACTIONS, OR DECIMALS **65**

Skill 8.1   Solve word problems involving integers, fractions, decimals, and
              percents... 65

Skill 8.2   Solve word problems involving ratios, and proportions..................... 65

COMPETENCY 9.0 INTERPRET INFORMATION FROM A GRAPH, TABLE OR CHART **68**

Skill 9.1   Interpret information in line graphs, bar graphs, pie graphs,
              pictographs, tables, charts, or graphs of functions. 68

COMPETENCY 10.0 GRAPH NUMBERS OR NUMBER RELATIONSHIPS **72**

Skill 10.1   Identify points from their coordinates, the coordinates of points, or
              graphs of sets of ordered pairs.. 72

Skill 10.2   Identify the graphs of equations or inequalities, and find the slopes
              and intercepts of lines.. 73

Skill 10.3   Recognize direct and inverse variation presented graphically........... 79

COMPETENCY 11.0 SOLVE ONE- AND TWO-VARIABLE EQUATIONS **81**

Skill 11.1   Find the value of the unknown in one-variable equations................. 81

Skill 11.2   Solve a system of two linear equations in two variables................... 82

COMPETENCY 12.0 SOLVE WORD PROBLEMS INVOLVING ONE AND TWO VARIABLES 84

Skill 12.1   Solve word problems that can be translated into one-variable linear equations or systems of two-variable linear equations. 84

COMPETENCY 13.0 UNDERSTAND OPERATIONS WITH ALGEBRAIC EXPRESSIONS 88

Skill 13.1   Factor quadratics and polynomials. 88

Skill 13.2   Add, subtract, and multiply polynomial expressions. 94

Skill 13.3   Perform basic operations on and simplifying rational expressions. ... 95

COMPETENCY 14.0 SOLVE PROBLEMS INVOLVING GEOMETRIC FIGURES 97

Skill 14.1   Identify the appropriate formula for solving geometric problems; solve problems involving two- and three-dimensional geometric figures. 97

Skill 14.2   Solve problems involving right triangles using the Pythagorean theorem. 107

COMPETENCY 15.0 APPLY REASONING SKILLS 109

Skill 15.1   Draw conclusions using the principles of similarity, congruence, parallelism, and perpendicularity. 109

Skill 15.2   Use inductive and deductive reasoning. 113

Sample Test: Mathematics 120

Answer Key 131

Answers with Rationale 132

DOMAIN III. WRITING 136

Great Study and Testing Tips!

What to study in order to prepare for the subject assessments is the focus of this study guide but equally important is *how* you study.

You can increase your chances of truly mastering the information by taking some simple, but effective steps.

Study Tips:

1. Some foods aid the learning process. Foods such as milk, nuts, seeds, rice, and oats help your study efforts by releasing natural memory enhancers called CCKs (*cholecystokinin*) composed of *tryptophan*, *choline*, and *phenylalanine*. All of these chemicals enhance the neurotransmitters associated with memory. Before studying, try a light, protein-rich meal of eggs, turkey, and fish. All of these foods release the memory enhancing chemicals. The better the connections, the more you comprehend.

Likewise, before you take a test, stick to a light snack of energy boosting and relaxing foods. A glass of milk, a piece of fruit, or some peanuts all release various memory-boosting chemicals and help you to relax and focus on the subject at hand.

2. Learn to take great notes. A by-product of our modern culture is that we have grown accustomed to getting our information in short doses (i.e. TV news sound bites or USA Today style newspaper articles.)

Consequently, we've subconsciously trained ourselves to assimilate information better in neat little packages. If your notes are scrawled all over the paper, it fragments the flow of the information. Strive for clarity. Newspapers use a standard format to achieve clarity. Your notes can be much clearer through use of proper formatting. A very effective format is called the *"Cornell Method."*

> Take a sheet of loose-leaf lined notebook paper and draw a line all the way down the paper about 1-2" from the left-hand edge.

> Draw another line across the width of the paper about 1-2" up from the bottom. Repeat this process on the reverse side of the page.

Look at the highly effective result. You have ample room for notes, a left hand margin for special emphasis items or inserting supplementary data from the textbook, a large area at the bottom for a brief summary, and a little rectangular space for just about anything you want.

3. <u>Get the concept then the details.</u> Too often we focus on the details and don't gather an understanding of the concept. However, if you simply memorize only dates, places, or names, you may well miss the whole point of the subject.

A key way to understand things is to put them in your own words. If you are working from a textbook, automatically summarize each paragraph in your mind. If you are outlining text, don't simply copy the author's words.

Rephrase them in your own words. You remember your own thoughts and words much better than someone else's, and subconsciously tend to associate the important details to the core concepts.

4. <u>Ask Why?</u> Pull apart written material paragraph by paragraph and don't forget the captions under the illustrations.

Example: If the heading is "Stream Erosion", flip it around to read "Why do streams erode?" Then answer the questions.

If you train your mind to think in a series of questions and answers, not only will you learn more, but it also helps to lessen the test anxiety because you are used to answering questions.

5. <u>Read for reinforcement and future needs.</u> Even if you only have 10 minutes, put your notes or a book in your hand. Your mind is similar to a computer; you have to input data in order to have it processed. *By reading, you are creating the neural connections for future retrieval.* The more times you read something, the more you reinforce the learning of ideas.

Even if you don't fully understand something on the first pass, *your mind stores much of the material for later recall.*

6. <u>Relax to learn so go into exile.</u> Our bodies respond to an inner clock called biorhythms. Burning the midnight oil works well for some people, but not everyone.

If possible, set aside a particular place to study that is free of distractions. Shut off the television, cell phone, pager and exile your friends and family during your study period.

If you really are bothered by silence, try background music. Light classical music at a low volume has been shown to aid in concentration over other types. Music that evokes pleasant emotions without lyrics are highly suggested. Try just about anything by Mozart. It relaxes you.

7. <u>Use arrows not highlighters.</u> At best, it's difficult to read a page full of yellow, pink, blue, and green streaks. Try staring at a neon sign for a while and you'll soon see that the horde of colors obscure the message.

A quick note, a brief dash of color, an underline, and an arrow pointing to a particular passage is much clearer than a horde of highlighted words.

8. Budget your study time. Although you shouldn't ignore any of the material, *allocate your available study time in the same ratio that topics may appear on the test.*

Testing Tips:

1. <u>**Get smart, play dumb.**</u> **Don't read anything into the question.** Don't make an assumption that the test writer is looking for something else than what is asked. Stick to the question as written and don't read extra things into it.

2. <u>**Read the question and all the choices *twice* before answering the question.**</u> You may miss something by not carefully reading, and then re-reading both the question and the answers.

If you really don't have a clue as to the right answer, leave it blank on the first time through. Go on to the other questions, as they may provide a clue as to how to answer the skipped questions.

If later on, you still can't answer the skipped ones . . . ***Guess.*** The only penalty for guessing is that you *might* get it wrong. Only one thing is certain; if you don't put anything down, you will get it wrong!

3. <u>**Turn the question into a statement.**</u> Look at the way the questions are worded. The syntax of the question usually provides a clue. Does it seem more familiar as a statement rather than as a question? Does it sound strange?

By turning a question into a statement, you may be able to spot if an answer sounds right, and it may also trigger memories of material you have read.

4. <u>**Look for hidden clues.**</u> It's actually very difficult to compose multiple-foil (choice) questions without giving away part of the answer in the options presented.

In most multiple-choice questions you can often readily eliminate one or two of the potential answers. This leaves you with only two real possibilities and automatically your odds go to Fifty-Fifty for very little work.

5. <u>**Trust your instincts.**</u> For every fact that you have read, you subconsciously retain something of that knowledge. On questions that you aren't really certain about, go with your basic instincts. **Your first impression on how to answer a question is usually correct.**

6. <u>**Mark your answers directly on the test booklet.**</u> Don't bother trying to fill in the optical scan sheet on the first pass through the test.

Be careful not to miss-mark your answers when you transcribe them to the scan sheet.

7. <u>**Watch the clock!**</u> You have a set amount of time to answer the questions. Don't get bogged down trying to answer a single question at the expense of 10 questions you can more readily answer.

DOMAIN I.   READING

COMPETENCY 1.0 DETERMINE THE MEANING OF WORDS AND PHRASES

Skill 1.1   **Use the context of a passage to determine the meaning of words with multiple meanings, unfamiliar and uncommon words and phrases, and figurative expressions.**

Context clues help readers determine the meaning of words they are not familiar with. The context of a word is the sentence or sentences that surround the word.

Read the following sentences and attempt to determine the meanings of the words in bold print.

> The **luminosity** of the room was so incredible that there was no need for lights.

If there was no need for lights then one must assume that the word luminosity has something to do with giving off light. The definition of luminosity is: the emission of light.

> Jamie could not understand Joe's feelings. His mood swings made understanding him somewhat of an **enigma.**

The fact that he could not be understood made him somewhat of a puzzle. The definition of enigma is: a mystery or puzzle.

Familiarity with word **roots** (the basic elements of words) and with **prefixes** can also help one determine the meanings of unknown words. Following is a partial list of roots and prefixes. It might be useful to review these.

Root	Meaning	Example
aqua	water	aqualung
astro	stars	astrology
bio	life	biology
carn	meat	carnivorous
circum	around	circumnavigate
geo	earth	geology
herb	plant	herbivorous
mal	bad	malicious
neo	new	neonatal
tele	distant	telescope

Prefix	Meaning	Example
un-	not	unnamed
re-	again	reenter
il-	not	illegible
pre-	before	preset
mis-	incorrectly	misstate
in-	not	informal
anti-	against	antiwar
de-	opposite	derail
post-	after	postwar
ir-	not	irresponsible

Word forms

Sometimes a very familiar word can appear as a different part of speech.

You may have heard that *fraud* involves a criminal misrepresentation, so when it appears as the adjective form *fraudulent* ("He was suspected of fraudulent activities") you can make an educated guess.

You probably know that something out of date is *obsolete;* therefore, when you read about "built-in *obsolescence,*" you can detect the meaning of the unfamiliar word.

Practice Questions: Read the following sentences and attempt to determine the meanings of the underlined words.

1.   Farmer John got a two-horse plow and went to work. Straight <u>furrows</u> stretched out behind him.

The word <u>furrows</u> means

    (A) long cuts made by plow
    (B) vast, open fields
    (C) rows of corn
    (D) pairs of hitched horses

2.   The survivors struggled ahead, <u>shambling</u> through the terrible cold, doing their best not to fall.

The word <u>shambling</u> means

    (A) frozen in place
    (B) running
    (C) shivering uncontrollably
    (D) walking awkwardly

Answers:

1. A. is the correct answer. The words "straight" and the expression "stretched out behind him" are your clues.

2. D. is the correct answer. The words "ahead" and "through" are your clues.

The context for a word is the written passage that surrounds it. Sometimes the writer offers synonyms—words that have nearly the same meaning. Context clues can appear within the sentence itself, within the preceding and/or following sentence(s), or in the passage as a whole.

Sentence clues

Often, a writer will actually **define** a difficult or particularly important word for you the first time it appears in a passage. Phrases like *that is, such as, which is,* or *is called* might announce the writer's intention to give just the definition you need. Occasionally, a writer will simply use a synonym (a word that means the same thing) or near-synonym joined by the word *or.* Look at the following examples:

> The credibility, that is to say the believability, of the witness was called into question by evidence of previous perjury.
> Nothing would assuage or lessen the child's grief.

Punctuation at the sentence level is often a clue to the meaning of a word. Commas, parentheses, quotation marks and dashes tell the reader that a definition is being offered by the writer.

> A tendency toward hyperbole, extravagant exaggeration, is a common flaw among persuasive writers.

> Political apathy - lack of interest - can lead to the death of the state.
A writer might simply give an **explanation** in other words that you can understand, in the same sentence:

> The xenophobic townspeople were suspicious of every foreigner.

Writers also explain a word in terms of its opposite at the sentence level:

> His incarceration was ended, and he was elated to be out of jail.

Adjacent sentence clues

The context for a word goes beyond the sentence in which it appears. At times, the writer uses adjacent (adjoining) sentences to present an explanation or definition:

> *The 200 dollars for the car repair would have to come out of the <u>contingency</u> fund. Fortunately, Angela's father had taught her to keep some money set aside for just such emergencies.*

Analysis: The second sentence offers a clue to the definition of *contingency* as used in this sentence: "emergencies." Therefore, a fund for contingencies would be money tucked away for unforeseen and/or urgent events.

Entire passage clues

On occasion, you must look at an entire paragraph or passage to figure out the definition of a word or term. In the following paragraph, notice how the word *nostalgia* undergoes a form of extended definition throughout the selection rather than in just one sentence.

> *The word <u>nostalgia</u> links Greek words for "away from home" and "pain." If you're feeling <u>nostalgic,</u> then, you are probably in some physical distress or discomfort, suffering from a feeling of alienation and separation from love ones or loved places. <u>Nostalgia</u> is that awful feeling you remember the first time you went away to camp or spent the weekend with a friend's family—homesickness, or some condition even more painful than that. But in common use, <u>nostalgia</u> has come to have more sentimental associations. A few years back, for example, a <u>nostalgia</u> craze had to do with the 1950s. We resurrected poodle skirts and saddle shoes, built new restaurants to look like old ones, and tried to make chicken a la king just as mother probably never made it. In TV situation comedies, we recreated a pleasant world that probably never existed and relished our <u>nostalgia,</u> longing for a homey, comfortable lost time.*

COMPETENCY 2.0 UNDERSTAND THE MAIN IDEA AND SUPPORTING DETAILS IN WRITTEN MATERIAL.

Skill 2.1   Identify explicit and implicit main ideas.

The main idea of a passage or paragraph is the basic message, idea, point concept, or meaning that the author wants to convey to you, the reader. Understanding the main idea of a passage or paragraph is the key to understanding the more subtle components of the author's message. The main idea is what is being said about a topic or subject. Once you have identified the basic message, you will have an easier time answering other questions that test critical skills.

Main ideas are either *stated* or *implied*. A *stated main idea* is explicit: it is directly expressed in a sentence or two in the paragraph or passage. An *implied main idea* is suggested by the overall reading selection. In the first case, you need not pull information from various points in the paragraph or passage in order to form the main idea because it is already stated by the author. If a main idea is implied, however, you must formulate, in your own words, a main idea statement by condensing the overall message contained in the material itself.

Practice Question: Read the following passage and select an answer

Sometimes too much of a good thing can become a very bad thing indeed. In an earnest attempt to consume a healthy diet, dietary supplement enthusiasts have been known to overdose. Vitamin C, for example, long thought to help people ward off cold viruses, is currently being studied for its possible role in warding off cancer and other disease that cases tissue degeneration. Unfortunately, an overdose of vitamin C – more than 10,000 mg – on a daily basis can cause nausea and diarrhea. Calcium supplements, commonly taken by women, are helpful in warding off osteoporosis. More than just a few grams a day, however, can lead to stomach upset and even kidney and bladder stones. Niacin, proven useful in reducing cholesterol levels, can be dangerous in large doses to those who suffer from heart problems, asthma or ulcers.

The main idea expressed in this paragraph is:

    A.   supplements taken in excess can be a bad thing indeed
    B.   dietary supplement enthusiasts have been known to overdose
    C.   vitamins can cause nausea, diarrhea, and kidney or bladder stones.
    D.   people who take supplements are preoccupied with their health.

Answer: Answer A is a paraphrase of the first sentence and provides a general framework for the rest of the paragraph: excess supplement intake is bad. The rest of the paragraph discusses the consequences of taking too many vitamins. Options B and C refer to major details, and Option D introduces the idea of preoccupation, which is not included in this paragraph.

Skill 2.2   Recognize ideas that support, illustrate, or elaborate the main idea of a passage

Supporting details are examples, facts, ideas, illustrations, cases and anecdotes used by a writer to explain, expand on, and develop the more general main idea. A writer's choice of supporting materials is determined by the nature of the topic being covered. Supporting details are specifics that relate directly to the main idea. Writers select and shape material according to their purposes. An advertisement writer seeking to persuade the reader to buy a particular running shoe, for instance will emphasize only the positive characteristics of the shoe for advertisement copy. A columnist for a running magazine, on the other hand, might list the good and bad points about the same shoe in an article recommending appropriate shoes for different kind of runners. Both major details (those that directly support the main idea), and minor details (those that provide interesting, but not always essential, information) help create a well-written and fluid passage.

In the following paragraph, the sentences in **bold print** provide a skeleton of a paragraph on the benefits of recycling. The sentences in bold are generalizations that by themselves do not explain the need to recycle. The sentences in *italics* add details to SHOW the general points in bold. Notice how the supporting details help you understand the necessity for recycling.

While one day recycling may become mandatory in all states, right now it is voluntary in many communities. *Those of us who participate in recycling are amazed by how much material is recycled.* **For many communities, the blue-box recycling program has had an immediate effect.** *By just recycling glass, aluminum cans, and plastic bottles, we have reduced the volume of disposable trash by one third, thus extending the useful life of local landfills by over a decade. Imagine the difference if those dramatic results were achieved nationwide.* **The amount of reusable items we thoughtlessly dispose of is staggering.** *For example, Americans dispose of enough steel everyday to supply Detroit car manufacturers for three months. Additionally, we dispose of enough aluminum annually to rebuild the nation's air fleet. These statistics, available from the Environmental Protection Agency (EPA), should encourage all of us to watch what we throw away.* **Clearly, recycling in our homes and in our communities directly improves the environment.**

Notice how the author's supporting examples enhance the message of the paragraph and relate to the author's thesis noted above. If you only read the bold-face sentences, you have a glimpse at the topic. This paragraph of, illustration, however, is developed through numerous details creating specific images: *reduced the volume of disposable trash by one-third; extended the useful life of local landfills by over a decade; enough steel everyday to supply Detroit car manufacturers for three months; enough aluminum to rebuild the nation's air fleet.* If the writer had merely written a few general sentences, as those shown in bold face, you would not fully understand the vast amount of trash involved in recycling or the positive results of current recycling efforts.

COMPETENCY 3.0 IDENTIFY A WRITER'S PURPOSE, POINT OF VIEW, AND INTENDED MEANING

Skill 3.1 Recognize a writer's expressed or implied purpose for writing.

An essay is an extended discussion of a writer's point of view about a particular topic. This point of view may be supported by using such writing modes as examples, argument and persuasion, analysis or comparison/contrast. in any case, a good essay is clear, coherent, well-organized and fully developed.

When an author sets out to write a passage, he/she usually has a purpose for doing so. That purpose may be to simply give information that might be interesting or useful to some reader or other; it may be to persuade the reader to a point of view or to move the reader to act in a particular way; it may be to tell a story; or it may be to describe something in such a way that an experience becomes available to the reader through one of the five senses. Following are the primary devices for expressing a particular purpose in a piece of writing:

- **Basic expository writing** simply gives information not previously known about a topic or is used to explain or define one. Facts, examples, statistics, cause and effect, direct tone, objective rather than subjective delivery, and non-emotional information is presented in a formal manner.

- **Descriptive writing** centers on person, place, or object, using concrete and sensory words to create a mood or impression and arranging details in a chronological or spatial sequence.

- **Narrative writing** is developed using an incident or anecdote or related series of events. Chronology, the 5 W's, topic sentence, and conclusion are essential ingredients.

- **Persuasive writing** implies the writer's ability to select vocabulary and arrange facts and opinions in such a way as to direct the actions of the listener/reader. Persuasive writing may incorporate exposition and narration as they illustrate the main idea.

- **Journalistic writing** is theoretically free of author bias. It is essential when relaying information about an event, person, or thing that it be factual and objective. Provide students with an opportunity to examine newspapers and create their own. Many newspapers have educational programs that are offered free to schools.

Skill 3.2 Evaluate the appropriateness of written material for various purposes or audiences.

Tailoring language for a particular **audience** is an important skill. Writing to be read by a business associate will surely sound different from writing to be read by a younger sibling. Not only are the vocabularies different, but the formality/informality of the discourse will need to be adjusted.

The things to be aware of in determining what the language should be for a particular audience, then, hinges on two things: **word choice** and formality/informality. The most formal language does not use contractions or slang. The most informal language will probably feature a more casual use of common sayings and anecdotes. Formal language will use longer sentences and will not sound like a conversation. The most informal language will use shorter sentences—not necessarily simple sentences—but shorter constructions and may sound like a conversation.

In both formal and informal writing there exists a **tone**, the writer's attitude toward the material and/or readers. Tone may be playful, formal, intimate, angry, serious, ironic, outraged, baffled, tender, serene, depressed, etc. The overall tone of a piece of writing is dictated by both the subject matter and the audience. Tone is also related to the actual words which make up the document, as we attach affective meanings to words, called **connotations**. Gaining this conscious control over language makes it possible to use language appropriately in various situations and to evaluate its uses in literature and other forms of communication. By evoking the proper responses from readers/listeners, we can prompt them to take action.

The following questions are an excellent way to assess the audience and tone of a given piece of writing.

1. Who is your audience? (friend, teacher, business person, someone else)
2. How much does this person know about you and/or your topic?
3. What is your purpose? (to prove an argument, to persuade, to amuse, to register a complaint, to ask for a raise, etc)
4. What emotions do you have about the topic? (nervous, happy, confident, angry, sad, no feelings at all)
5. What emotions do you want to register with your audience? (anger, nervousness, happiness, boredom, interest)
6. What persona do you need to create in order to achieve your purpose?
7. What choice of language is best suited to achieving your purpose with your particular subject? (slang, friendly but respectful, formal)
8. What emotional quality do you want to transmit to achieve your purpose (matter of fact, informative, authoritative, inquisitive, sympathetic, angry) and to what degree do you want to express this tone?

Skill 3.3 **Recognize the likely effect of a writer's choice of words on an audience.**

See Skill 3.2.

Skill 3.4 **Use the content, word choice, and phrasing of a passage to determine a writer's opinion or point of view.**

The **tone** of a written passage is the author's attitude toward the subject matter. The tone (mood, feeling) is revealed through the qualities of the writing itself and is a direct product of such stylistic elements as language and sentence structure. The tone of the written passage is much like a speaker's voice; instead of being spoken, however, it is the product of words on a page.

Often, writers have an emotional stake in the subject; and their purpose, either explicitly or implicitly, is to convey those feelings to the reader. In such cases, the writing is generally subjective: that is, it stems from opinions, judgments, values, ideas, and feelings. Both sentence structure (syntax) and word choice (diction) are instrumental tools in creating tone.

Tone may be thought of generally as positive, negative, or neutral. Below is a statement about snakes that demonstrates this.

> *Many species of snakes live in Florida. Some of those species, both poisonous and non-poisonous, have habitats that coincide with those of human residents of the state.*

The voice of the writer in this statement is neutral. The sentences are declarative (not exclamations or fragments or questions). The adjectives are few and nondescript—*many, some, poisonous* (balanced with *non -poisonous*). Nothing much in this brief paragraph would alert the reader to the feelings of the writer about snakes. The paragraph has a neutral, objective, detached, impartial tone.

Then again, if the writer's attitude toward snakes involves admiration or even affection the tone would generally be positive:

> *Florida's snakes are a tenacious bunch. When they find their habitats invaded by humans, they cling to their home territories as long as they can, as if vainly attempting to fight off the onslaught of the human hordes.*

An additional message emerges in this paragraph: The writer quite clearly favors snakes over people. The writer uses adjectives like *tenacious* to describe his/her feelings about snakes. The writer also humanizes the reptiles, making them brave, beleaguered creatures. Obviously the writer is more sympathetic to snakes than to people in this paragraph.

If the writer's attitude toward snakes involves active dislike and fear, then the tone would also reflect that attitude by being negative:

> *Countless species of snakes, some more dangerous than others, still lurk on the urban fringes of Florida's towns and cities. They will often invade domestic spaces, terrorizing people and their pets.*

Here, obviously, the snakes are the villains. They *lurk,* they *invade,* and they *terrorize.* The tone of this paragraph might be said to be distressed about snakes.

In the same manner, a writer can use language to portray characters as good or bad. A writer uses positive and negative adjectives, as seen above, to convey the manner of a character.

COMPETENCY 4.0 ANALYZE THE RELATIONSHIP AMONG IDEAS IN WRITTEN MATERIAL

Skill 4.1   Identify the sequence of events or steps

The ability to organize events or steps provided in a passage (especially when presented in random order) serves a useful purpose, and it encourages the development of logical thinking and the processes of analysis and evaluation.

Working through and discussing with your students examples like the one below help students to gain valuable practice in sequencing events.

Practice Question: identify the proper order of events or steps.

1. Matt had tied a knot in his shoelace.
2. Matt put on his green socks because they were clean and complimented the brown slacks he was wearing.
3. Matt took a bath and trimmed his toenails.
4. Matt put on his brown slacks.

Answer: The proper order of events is: 3, 4, 2, and 1

Skill 4.2   Identify cause-effect relationships

A cause is the necessary source of a particular outcome. If a writer were addressing the question "How will the new tax laws affect small businesses?" or "Why has there been such political unrest in Somalia?" he or she would use cause and effect as an organizational pattern to structure their response. In the first case, the writer would emphasize effects of the tax legislation as they apply to owners of small businesses. In the second, they would focus on causes for the current political situation in Somalia.

Some word clues that identify a cause-effect passage are: accordingly, as a result, therefore, because, consequently, hence, in short, thus, then, due to and so on.

Sample passage:
Simply put, inflation is an increase in price levels. It happens when a government prints more currency than is already in circulation, and there is, consequently, additional money available for the same amount of good or services. There might be multiple reasons for a government to crank up the printing presses. A war, for instance, could cause an immediate need for steel. A national disaster might create a sudden need for social services. To get the money it needs, a government can raise taxes, borrow, or print more currency. However, raising taxes and borrowing are not always plausible options.

Analysis: The paragraph starts with a definition and proceeds to examine a causal chain. The words *consequently*, *reasons* and *cause* provide the clues.

Explicit Cause and Effect

General Hooker failed to anticipate General Lee's bold flanking maneuver. As a result, Hooker's army was nearly routed by a smaller force.

Mindy forgot to bring the lunch her father had packed for her. Consequently, she had to borrow money from her friends at school during lunch period.

Implicit Cause and Effect

The engine in Lisa's airplane began to sputter. She quickly looked below for a field in which to land.

Luther ate the creamed shrimp that had been sitting in the sun for hours. Later that night, he was so sick he had to be rushed to the hospital.

Skill 4.3   Analyze relationships between ideas in opposition.

Whenever there are two ideas in opposition there is the ghost of an "either/or" conceptual basis lurking invisibly in the background of the "pro/con" setting.

For example, one person may argue that automobiles are a safer mode of transportation than are motorcycles and support that contention with statistics showing that fatalities are more frequent per accident in motorcycle crashes than in car crashes.

The opposition to this argument may counter that while fatalities are more frequent per accident in motorcycle accidents, it is erroneous to over generalize from that statistic that motorcycles are "therefore more dangerous."

Thus, each participant in the argument has assumed a position of "either or," that is to say, the automobile is "either" safer than the motorcycle, or it is not (or the motorcycle is "either" safer than the automobile or it is not). With the argument thus formulated, a conclusion acceptable to both sides is not likely to happen.

Here is a short essay showing how to avoid this deadlock.

Which is safer? The car or the motorcycle?

Most experienced drivers would agree that while it is more exhilarating to ride a motorcycle than to drive an automobile, it is illogical to therefore conclude that this exhilaration leads to careless driving and, therefore, more accidents, deaths, and injuries to motorcycle readers than car drivers. The critical concept to be understood here is not exhilaration, which is a given, but how the exhilaration comes about and is a cause of serious injury and death of motorcycle riders.

There is safe and unsafe thrill seeking. "Exhilaration" is defined as the "state of being stimulated, refreshed, or elated". An example of safe exhilaration is the excitement of sledding downhill, which results in the sled rider feeling stimulated, refreshed, and/or elated.

Unsafe exhilaration, which is usually the consequence of reckless thrill seeking, is therefore a state of being over-stimulated, frightened, and depressed by terror.

Which then causes more dangerous exhilaration, the car or the motorcycle? The answer is that the two forms of exhilaration are the consequents not of the motorcycle or the automobile, per se, but of the operation of the respective vehicles. Without an operator, both vehicles are metal entities, sitting in space, neither threatening nor harmful to anyone.

Therefore, neither the motorcycle nor the car is more, or less dangerous than one another: it is the attitude of their operators that creates the danger, death, and dismemberment resultant from accidents.

Notice how the writer has avoided the logical trap of the "either/or" construction built into the "pro con" argument by defining the key term "exhilaration" to clarify the issue (and shift the focus to the operator) and resolve the either/or dilemma BY arguing that it is the operators of the vehicles that are responsible for negative consequences, not the vehicles themselves.

Skill 4.4   Identify solutions to problems.

Within the assessment of reading, working with more than one selection is important in deciding if students can make generalizations. Utilizing the information read to find the answer to a situation presented is the skill. Sometimes this may involve problems specifically identified within what was read. For example, the characters in the story may be having a specific problem, like a lack of money. Then as you continue to read the passage the characters in the story were hired for a new job, which allowed them to earn more money. Using the information read, identify the problem (a lack of money) and the solution (a new job).

In other cases, generalizations will need to be made across multiple selections. In those cases selecting problems and solutions may be more evasive. Problems and solutions across texts will require broader thinking. The problems and solutions will not be as clearly spelled out in the text. It will involve you thinking on a different level about how the two passages relate. Connecting texts to other texts and finding common elements within them allows you to then draw out the common problems and solutions. Working through multiple selections requires more complex thinking skills and thinking of problems and solutions sometimes in other terms. Perhaps thinking of the challenge or issue that was faced and how that issue was overcome would help to broaden the scope and understanding of identifying the common problem and therefore the solution.

Skill 4.5   Draw conclusions inductively and deductively from information stated or implied in a passage.

An **inference** is sometimes called an "educated guess" because it requires that you go beyond the strictly obvious to create additional meaning by taking the text one logical step further. Inferences and conclusions are based on the content of the passage – that is, on what the passage says or how the writer says it – and are derived by reasoning.

Inference is an essential and automatic component of most reading. For example, in making educated guesses about the meaning of unknown words, the author's main idea or whether he or she is writing with a bias. Such is the essence of inference: you use your own ability to reason in order to figure out what the writer implies. As a reader, then, you must often logically extend meaning that is only implied.

Consider the following example. Assume you are an employer, and you are reading over the letters of reference submitted by a prospective employee for the position of clerk/typist in your real estate office. The position requires the applicant to be neat, careful, trustworthy, and punctual. You come across this letter of reference submitted by an applicant:

To whom it may concern,

Todd Finley has asked me to write a letter of reference for him. I am well qualified to do so because he worked for me for three months last year. His duties included answering the phone, greeting the public, and producing some simple memos and notices on the computer. Although Todd initially had few computer skills and little knowledge of telephone etiquette, he did acquire some during his stay with us. Todd's manner of speaking, both on the telephone and with the clients who came to my establishment, could be described as casual. He was particularly effective when communicating with peers. Please contact me by telephone if you wish to have further information about my experience.

Here the writer implies, rather than openly states, the main idea. This letter calls attention to itself because there's a problem with its tone. A truly positive letter would say something like "I have distinct honor to recommend Todd Finley." Here, however, the letter simply verifies that Todd worked in the office. Second, the praise is obviously lukewarm. For example, the writer says that Todd "was particularly effective when communicating with peers." And educated guess translates that statement into a nice way of saying Todd was not serious about his communication with clients.

In order to draw **inferences** and make **conclusions**, a reader must use prior knowledge and apply it to the current situation. A conclusion or inference is never stated. You must rely on your common sense.

Practice Questions: Read the following passages and select an answer

1. The Smith family waited patiently around carousel number 7 for their luggage to arrive. They were exhausted after their 5 hour trip and were anxious to get to their hotel. After about an hour, they realized that they no longer recognized any of the other passengers' faces. Mrs. Smith asked the person who appeared to be in charge if they were at the right carousel. The man replied, "Yes, this is it, but we finished unloading that baggage almost half an hour ago."

    From the man's response we can infer that:
    (A) The Smiths were ready to go to their hotel.
    (B) The Smith's luggage was lost.
    (C) The man had their luggage.
    (D) They were at the wrong carousel.

2. Tim Sullivan had just turned 15. As a birthday present, his parents had given him a guitar and a certificate for 10 guitar lessons. He had always shown a love of music and a desire to learn an instrument. Tim began his lessons and before long, he was making up his own songs. At the music studio, Tim met Josh, who played the piano and Roger, whose instrument was the saxophone. They all shared the same dream, to start a band and each was praised by his teacher as having real talent.

    From this passage one can infer that
    (A) Tim, Roger & Josh are going to start their own band.
    (B) Tim is going to give up his guitar lessons.
    (C) Tim, Josh & Roger will no longer be friends.
    (D) Josh & Roger are going to start their own band.

Answers:

1. Since the Smiths were still waiting for their luggage, we know that they were not yet ready to go to their hotel. From the man's response, we know that they were not at the wrong carousel and that he did not have their luggage. Therefore, though not directly stated, it appears that their luggage was lost. Choice (B) is the correct answer.

2. (A) is the correct choice. Given the facts that Tim wanted to be a musician and start his own band, after meeting others who shared the same dreams, we can infer that they joined together in an attempt to make their dreams become a reality.

COMPETENCY 5.0 USE CRITICAL REASONING SKILLS TO EVALUATE WRITTEN MATERIAL

Skill 5.1   **Evaluate the stated or implied assumptions on which the validity of a writer's argument depends.**

On the test, the terms **valid** and invalid have special meaning. If an argument is valid, it is reasonable. It is objective (not biased) and can be supported by evidence. If an argument is invalid, it is not reasonable. It is not objective. In other words, one can find evidence of bias.

Practice Questions: Read the following passages and select an answer.

1.   Most dentists agree that Bright Smile Toothpaste is the best for fighting cavities. It tastes good and leaves your mouth minty fresh.

   Is this a valid or invalid argument?

   (A) valid
   (B) invalid

2.   It is difficult to decide who will make the best presidential candidate, Senator Johnson or Senator Keeley. They have both been involved in scandals and have both gone through messy divorces while in office.

   Is this argument valid or invalid?

   (A) valid
   (B) invalid

Answers:

1. It is invalid B. It mentions that "most" dentists agree. What about those who do not agree? The author is clearly exhibiting bias in leaving those who disagree out.

2. A. is the correct choice. The author appears to be listing facts. He does not seem to favor one candidate over the other.

Skill 5.2   Judge the relevance or importance of facts, examples, or graphic data to a writer's argument.

It is important to continually assess whether or not a sentence contributes to the overall task of supporting the main idea. When a sentence is deemed irrelevant it is best to either omit it from the passage or to make it relevant by one of the following strategies:

1. Adding detail – Sometimes a sentence can seem out of place if it does not contain enough information to link it to the topic. Adding specific information can show how the sentence is related to the main idea.

2. Adding an example – This is especially important in passages in which information is being argued or compared or contrasted. Examples can support the main idea and give the document overall credibility.

3. Using diction effectively – It is important to understand connotation, avoid ambiguity, and steer clear of too much repetition when selecting words.

4. Adding transitions – Transitions are extremely helpful for making sentences relevant because they are specifically designed to connect one idea to another. They can also reduce a paragraphs choppiness.

Skill 5.3   Evaluate the logic of a writer's argument.

An argument is a generalization that is proven or supported with facts. If the facts are not accurate, the generalization remains unproven. Using inaccurate "facts" to support an argument is called a *fallacy* in reasoning. Some factors to consider in judging whether the facts used to support an argument are accurate are as follow:

1. Are the facts current or are they out of date? For example, if the proposition "birth defects in babies born to drug-using mothers are increasing," then the data must include the latest that is available.
2. Another important factor to consider in judging the accuracy of a fact is its source. Where was the data obtained, and is that source reliable?
3. The calculations on which the facts are based may be unreliable. It's a good idea to run one's own calculations before using a piece of derived information.

Even facts that are true and have a sharp impact on the argument may not be relevant to the case at hand.

1. Health statistics from an entire state may have no relevance, or little relevance, to a particular county or zip code. Statistics from an entire country cannot be used to prove very much about a particular state or county.
2. An analogy can be useful in making a point, but the comparison must match up in all characteristics or it will not be relevant. Analogy should be used very carefully. It is often just as likely to destroy an argument as it is to strengthen it.

The importance or significance of a fact may not be sufficient to strengthen an argument. For example, of the millions of immigrants in the U.S., using a single family to support a solution to the immigration problem will not make much difference overall even though those single-example arguments are often used to support one approach or another. They may achieve a positive reaction, but they will not prove that one solution is better than another. If enough cases were cited from a variety of geographical locations, the information might be significant. How much is enough? Generally speaking, three strong supporting facts are sufficient to establish the thesis of an argument. For example:

Conclusion: All green apples are sour.
- When I was a child, I bit into a green apple from my grandfather's orchard, and it was sour.
- I once bought green apples from a roadside vendor, and when I bit into one, it was sour.
- My grocery store had a sale on green Granny Smith apples last week, and I bought several only to find that they were sour when I bit into one.

The fallacy in the above argument is that the sample was insufficient. A more exhaustive search of literature, etc., will probably turn up some green apples that are not sour.

A very good example of the omission of facts in an argument is the résumé of an applicant for a job. The applicant is arguing that he/she should be chosen to be awarded a particular job. The application form will ask for information about past employment, and unfavorable dismissals from jobs in the past may just be omitted. Employers are usually suspicious of periods of time when the applicant has not listed an employer.

A writer makes choices about which facts will be used and which will be discarded in developing an argument. Those choices may exclude anything that is not supportive of the point of view the arguer is taking. It's always a good idea for the reader to do some research to spot the omissions and to ask whether they have impact on acceptance of the point of view presented in the argument. No judgment is either black or white. If the argument seems too neat or too compelling, there are probably facts that might be relevant that have not been included.

Skill 5.4   Evaluate the validity of analogies.

An argument by analogy states that if two things have one thing in common they probably have other things in common. For example, peaches and plums are both fruits that have chemicals good for people to eat. Both peaches and plums are circular in shape; thus, it could be argued by analogy that "because" something is circular in shape it is fruit and something good for people to eat. However, this analogical deduction is not logical (for example, a baseball is circular in shape but hardly good to eat).

An analogy is a comparison of the likenesses of two things. The danger of arguing by analogy rests in a failure to correctly perceive the limitations of the likenesses between the two things compared. Because something is like something else does not make it the same as the compared object or, for that matter, put it in the same class as the original object.

For example a false argument based on analogical thinking could go like this: "Blake and Blunder are both democrats. Both are married. Both have three children, a dog, and a kitten at home. Therefore, it is likely they will both vote the same way about the school mileage proposal because of their similarities."

This is a false argument by analogy: while the likenesses cited are somewhat striking, these are only likenesses coincidental in nature, and not compelling causative roots predictive of behaviors.

However, perceiving the analogical relationship between two things or phenomena is often also the starting point for scientific investigations of reality and such perceptions are the subjects of a host of scientific theories (i.e., the work of Charles Darwin) and investigations (i.e., "wave/particle" theories in quantum physics). Such analogical relations require austere scrutiny and analysis and without such are essentially meaningless or the stuff of poetic comparisons ("To see the world in a grain of sand"-William Blake).

Thinking in analogies is the way we all began as children to perceive the world and sort it into categories of "good and bad" ("water is a liquid that is good for me, hot oil is a liquid that is bad for me"). Mature writers and thinkers discriminate carefully between all elements of an argument by analogy.

Skill 5.5   Distinguish between fact and opinion.

Facts are statements that are verifiable. Opinions are statements that must be supported in order to be accepted such as beliefs, values, judgments or feelings. Facts are objective statements used to support subjective opinions. For example, "Jane is a bad girl" is an opinion. However, "Jane hit her sister with a baseball bat" is a *fact* upon which the opinion is based. Judgments are opinions—decisions or declarations based on observation or reasoning that express approval or disapproval. Facts report what has happened or exists and come from observation, measurement, or calculation. Facts can be tested and verified whereas opinions and judgments cannot. They can only be supported with facts.

Most statements cannot be so clearly distinguished. "I believe that Jane is a bad girl" is a fact. The speaker knows what he/she believes. However, it obviously includes a judgment that could be disputed by another person who might believe otherwise. Judgments are not usually so firm. They are, rather, plausible opinions that provoke thought or lead to factual development.

Joe DiMaggio, a Yankees' center-fielder, was replaced by Mickey Mantle in 1952.
This is a fact. If necessary, evidence can be produced to support this.

First year players are more ambitious than seasoned players.
This is an opinion. There is no proof to support that everyone feels this way

Practice Questions: Decide if the statement is fact or opinion

1. The Inca were a group of Indians who ruled an empire in South America.

   (A) fact
   (B) opinion

2. The Inca were clever.

   (A) fact
   (B) opinion

3. The Inca built very complex systems of bridges.

   (A) fact
   (B) opinion

Answers:

1. A. is the correct answer. Research can prove this to be true.
2. B. is the correct answer. It is doubtful that all people who have studied the Inca agree with this statement. Therefore, no proof is available.
3. A. is the correct answer. As with question number one, research can prove this to be true.

Skill 5.6   Assess the credibility or objectivity of the writer or source of written material.

Bias is defined as an opinion, feeling or influence that strongly favors one side in an argument. A statement or passage is biased if an author attempts to convince a reader of something.

Is there evidence of bias in the following statement?

Using a calculator cannot help a student understand the process of graphing, so its use is a waste of time.

Since the author makes it perfectly clear that he does not favor the use of the calculator in graphing problem, the answer is yes, there is evidence of bias. He has included his opinion in this statement.

Practice Question: Read the following paragraph and select an answer

There are teachers who feel that computer programs are quite helpful in helping students grasp certain math concepts. There are also those who disagree with this feeling. It is up to each individual math teacher to decide if computer programs benefit her particular group of students.

Is there evidence of bias in this paragraph?
(A) yes
(B) no

Answer:

B. is the correct answer. The author seems to state both sides of the argument without favoring a particular side.

The sky is blue", "the sky looks like rain", one a fact and the other an opinion. This is because one is **readily provable by objective empirical data**, while the other is a **subjective evaluation based upon personal bias**. This means that facts are things that can be proved by the usual means of study and experimentation. We can look and see the color of the sky. Since the shade we are observing is expressed as the color blue and is an accepted norm, the observation that the sky is blue is therefore a fact. (Of course, this depends on other external factors such as time and weather conditions).

This brings us to our next idea: that it looks like rain. This is a subjective observation in that an individual's perception will differ from another. What looks like rain to one person will not necessarily look like that to another person. The question thus remains as to how to differentiate fact from opinion. The best and only way is to ask oneself if what is being stated can be proved from other sources, by other methods, or by the simple process of **reasoning**.

Primary and secondary sources

The resources used to support a piece of writing can be divided into two major groups: primary sources and secondary sources.

Primary sources are works, records, etc. that were created during the period being studied or immediately after it. Secondary sources are works written significantly after the period being studied and based upon primary sources. Primary sources are the basic materials that provide raw data and information. Secondary sources are the works that contain the explications of, and judgments on, this primary material.

Primary sources include the following kinds of materials:

- Documents that reflect the immediate, everyday concerns of people: memoranda, bills, deeds, charters, newspaper reports, pamphlets, graffiti, popular writings, journals or diaries, records of decision-making bodies, letters, receipts, snapshots, etc.
- Theoretical writings which reflect care and consideration in composition and an attempt to convince or persuade. The topic will generally be deeper and more pervasive values than is the case with "immediate" documents. These may include newspaper or magazine editorials, sermons, political speeches, philosophical writings, etc.
- Narrative accounts of events, ideas, trends, etc. written with intentionality by someone contemporary with the events described.
- Statistical data, although statistics may be misleading.
- Literature and nonverbal materials, novels, stories, poetry and essays from the period, as well as coins, archaeological artifacts, and art produced during the period.

Secondary sources include the following kinds of materials:

- Books written on the basis of primary materials about the period of time.
- Books written on the basis of primary materials about persons who played a major role in the events under consideration.
- Books and articles written on the basis of primary materials about the culture, the social norms, the language, and the values of the period.
- Quotations from primary sources.
- Statistical data on the period.
- The conclusions and inferences of other historians.
- Multiple interpretations of the ethos of the time.

Guidelines for the use of secondary sources:

1. Do not rely upon only a single secondary source.
2. Check facts and interpretations against primary sources whenever possible.
3. Do not accept the conclusions of other historians uncritically.
4. Place greatest reliance on secondary sources created by the best and most respected scholars.
5. Do not use the inferences of other scholars as if they were facts.
6. Ensure that you recognize any bias the writer brings to his/her interpretation of history.
7. Understand the primary point of the book as a basis for evaluating the value of the material presented in it to your questions.

COMPETENCY 6.0 APPLY STUDY SKILLS TO READING ASSIGNMENTS

Skill 6.1   Organize and summarize information for study purposes.

Sample Passage
Chili peppers may turn out to be the wonder drug of the decade. the fiery fruit comes in many sizes, shapes and colors, all of which grow on plants that are genetic descendants of the tepin plant, originally native to the Americas. Connoisseurs of the regional cuisines of the South west and Louisiana are already well aware that food flavored with chilies can cause a good sweat, but medical researchers are learning more every day about the medical power of capsaicin, the ingredient in the peppers that produces the heat.

Capsaicin as a pain medication has been a part of fold medicine for centuries. It is, in fact, the active ingredient in several currently available over-the-counter liniments for sore muscles. Recent research has been examining the value of the compound for the treatment of other painful conditions. Capsaicin shows some promise in the treatment of phantom limb syndrome, as well as shingles, and some types of headaches. Additional research focuses upon the use of capsaicin to relieve pain in post-surgical patients. Scientists speculate that application of the compound to the skin cause the body to release endorphins – natural pain relievers manufactured by the body itself. An alternative theory holds that capsaicin somehow interferes with t transmission of signals along the nerve fibers, thus reducing the sensation of pain.

In addition to its well0documented history as a pain killer, capsaicin has recently received attention as a phytochemical, one of the naturally occurring compounds from foods that show cancer-fighting qualities. Like the phytochemical sulfoaphane found in broccoli, capsaicin might turn out to be an agent capable of short-circuiting the actions of carcinogens at the cell level before they can cause cancer.

Summary: Chili peppers contain a chemical called capsaicin which has proved useful for treating a variety of ailments. Recent research reveals that capsaicin is a phytochemical, a natural compound that may help fight cancer.

Outline: -Chili peppers could be the wonder drug of the decade
-Chili peppers contains capsaicin
-Capsaicin can be used as a pain medication
-Capsaicin is a phytochemical
-Phytochemicals show cancer-fighting qualities
-Capsaicin might be able to short-circuit the effects of carcinogens

Skill 6.2   Follow written instructions or directions.

Step by Step

How does one get from here to there, from kindergarten to graduate school or to a trade school? The answer of course is by one step at a time, by carefully organizing one's courses of action, each phase building on the previous step and leading to the next.

Similarly, when taking a test you are asked to follow written instructions or directions the examiner wants to see how you manage your answer to the exam question. How do you organize your answer logically? How do you support your conclusions? How well connected are your ideas and the support you bring to your argument?

Look at how the writer does these tasks in the following essay:

Parenting Classes

Someone once said that the two most difficult jobs in the world - voting and being a parent - are given to rank amateurs. The consequences of this inequity are voter apathy and inept parenting leading to, on the one hand, an apparent failure of the democratic process and, on the other hand, misbehaving and misguided children.

The antidote for the first problem is in place in most school systems. Classes in history, civics, history, government, and student government provide a kind of "hands on" training in becoming an active member of society so that the step from student hood to citizenship is clear and expected.

On the other hand, most school systems in the past have avoided or given only lip service to the issue of parenting and parenting skills. The moral issue of illegitimate births aside, the reality of the world is that each year there are large numbers of children born to unwed parents who have had little, or no, training in child rearing.

What was done on the farm in the past is irrelevant here: the farm is gone and/or has been replaced by the inner city, and the pressing issue is how to train uneducated new parents in the child rearing tasks before them. Other issues are secondary to the immediate needs of newborns and their futures. And it is in their futures that the quality of life for all of us is found.

Thus, while we can debate this issue all we wish, we cannot responsibly ignore that uneducated parents need to be educated in the tasks before them, and it is clear that the best way to do this is in the school system, where these new parents are already learning how to be responsible citizens in the civics and other classes currently in place.

Notice how the writer moves sequentially from one idea to the next, maintaining throughout the parallel of citizenship and parenthood, from the opening quotation, paragraph by paragraph to the concluding sentence. Each idea is developed from the preceding idea, and each new idea refers to the preceding ideas, and at no point do related, but irrelevant issues sidetrack the writer.

Skill 6.3 **Interpret information presented in charts, graphs, or tables.**

See Skill 9.1.

Sample Test: Reading

Read the passages and answer the questions that follow.

This writer has often been asked to tutor hospitalized children with cystic fibrosis. While undergoing all the precautionary measures to see these children (i.e. scrubbing thoroughly and donning sterilized protective gear- for the child's protection), she has often wondered why their parents subject these children to the pressures of schooling and trying to catch up on what they have missed because of hospitalization, which is a normal part of cystic fibrosis patients' lives. These children undergo so many tortuous treatments a day that it seems cruel to expect them to learn as normal children do, especially with their life expectancies being as short as they are.

1. **What is meant by the word "precautionary" in the second sentence?**

    A.   Careful
    B.   Protective
    C.   Medical
    D.   Sterilizing

2. **What is the author's tone?**

    A.   Sympathetic
    B.   Cruel
    C.   Disbelieving
    D.   Cheerful

3. **What is the main idea of this passage?**

    A.   There is a lot of preparation involved in visiting a patient of cystic fibrosis.
    B.   Children with cystic fibrosis are incapable of living normal lives.
    C.   Certain concessions should be made for children with cystic fibrosis.
    D.   Children with cystic fibrosis die young.

4. **How is the author so familiar with the procedures used when visiting a child with cystic fibrosis?**

    A.   She has read about it.
    B.   She works in a hospital.
    C.   She is the parent of one.
    D.   She often tutors them.

5. **What is the author's purpose?**

    A.   To inform
    B.   To entertain
    C.   To describe
    D.   To narrate

6. **What type of organizational pattern is the author using?**

   A. Classification
   B. Explanation
   C. Comparison and contrast
   D. Cause and effect

7. **The author states that it is "cruel" to expect children with cystic fibrosis to learn as "normal" children do. Is this a fact or an opinion?**

   A. Fact
   B. Opinion

8. **Is there evidence of bias in this paragraph?**

   A. Yes
   B. No

9. **What kind of relationship is found within the last sentence which starts with "These children undergo..." and ends with "...as short as they are"?**

   A. Addition
   B. Explanation
   C. Generalization
   D. Classification

10. **Does the author present an argument that is valid or invalid concerning the schooling of children with cystic fibrosis?**

    A. Valid
    B. Invalid

Disciplinary practices have been found to affect diverse areas of child development such as the acquisition of moral values, obedience to authority, and performance at school. Even though the dictionary has a specific definition of the word "discipline," it is still open to interpretation by people of different cultures.

There are four types of disciplinary styles: assertion of power, withdrawal of love, reasoning, and permissiveness. Assertion of power involves the use of force to discourage unwanted behavior. Withdrawal of love involves making the love of a parent conditional on a child's good behavior. Reasoning involves persuading the child to behave one way rather than another. Permissiveness involves allowing the child to do as he or she pleases and face the consequences of his/her actions.

11. **What is the meaning of the word "diverse" in the first sentence?**

   A. Many
   B. Related to children
   C. Disciplinary
   D. Moral

12. **What organizational structure is used in the first sentence of the second paragraph?**

   A. Addition
   B. Explanation
   C. Definition
   D. Simple listing

13. **Name the four types of disciplinary styles.**

   A. Reasoning, power assertion, morality, and permissiveness.
   B. Morality, reasoning, permissiveness, and withdrawal of love.
   C. Withdrawal of love, permissiveness, assertion of power, and reasoning.
   D. Permissiveness, morality, reasoning, and power assertion.

14. **What is the main idea of this passage?**

   A. Different people have different ideas of what discipline is.
   B. Permissiveness is the most widely used disciplinary style.
   C. Most people agree on their definition of discipline.
   D. There are four disciplinary styles.

15. **What is the author's purpose in writing this?**

   A. To describe
   B. To narrate
   C. To entertain
   D. To inform

16. **Is this passage biased?**

   A. Yes
   B. No

17. **What is the author's tone?**

   A. Disbelieving
   B. Angry
   C. Informative
   D. Optimistic

18. **What is the overall organizational pattern of this passage?**

   A. Generalization
   B. Cause and effect
   C. Addition
   D. Summary

19. **The author states that "assertion of power involves the use of force to discourage unwanted behavior." Is this a fact or an opinion?**

   A. Fact
   B. Opinion

20. **From reading this passage we can conclude that**

   A. The author is a teacher.
   B. The author has many children.
   C. The author has written a book about discipline.
   D. The author has done a lot of research on discipline.

21. **What does the technique of reasoning involve?**

   A. Persuading the child to behave in a certain way.
   B. Allowing the child to do as he/she pleases.
   C. Using force to discourage unwanted behavior.
   D. Making love conditional on good behavior.

One of the most difficult problems plaguing American education is the assessment of teachers. No one denies that teachers ought to be answerable for what they do, but what exactly does that mean? The Oxford American Dictionary defines accountability as: the obligation to give a reckoning or explanation for one's actions.

Does a student have to learn for teaching to have taken place? Historically, teaching has not been defined in this restrictive manner; the teacher was thought to be responsible for the quantity and quality of material covered and the way in which it was presented. However, some definitions of teaching now imply that students must learn in order for teaching to have taken place.

As a teacher who tries my best to keep current on all the latest teaching strategies, I believe that those teachers who do not bother even to pick up an educational journal every once in a while should be kept under close watch. There are many teachers out there who have been teaching for decades and refuse to change their ways even if research has proven that their methods are outdated and ineffective. There is no place in the profession of teaching for these types of individuals. It is time that the American educational system clean house, for the sake of our children.

22. **What is the meaning of the word "reckoning" in the third sentence?**

A. Thought
B. Answer
C. Obligation
D. Explanation

23. **What is the organizational pattern of the second paragraph?**

A. Cause and effect
B. Classification
C. Addition
D. Explanation

24. **What is the main idea of the passage?**

A. Teachers should not be answerable for what they do.
B. Teachers who do not do their job should be fired.
C. The author is a good teacher.
D. Assessment of teachers is a serious problem in society today.

25. **Is this a valid argument?**

A. Yes
B. No

26. **From the passage, one can infer that**

A. The author considers herself a good teacher.
B. Poor teachers will be fired.
C. Students have to learn for teaching to take place.
D. The author will be fired.

27. **Teachers who do not keep current on educational trends should be fired. Is this a fact or an opinion?**

A. Fact
B. Opinion

28. **The author states that teacher assessment is a problem for**

A. Elementary schools
B. Secondary schools
C. American education
D. Families

29. **What is the author's purpose in writing this?**

A. To entertain
B. To narrate
C. To describe
D. To persuade

30. **Is there evidence of bias in this passage?**

A. Yes
B. No

31. **What is the author's overall organizational pattern?**

A. Classification
B. Cause and effect
C. Definition
D. Comparison and contrast

32. **The author's tone is one of**

A. Disbelief
B. Excitement
C. Support
D. Concern

33. **What is meant by the word "plaguing" in the first sentence?**

A. Causing problems
B. Causing illness
C. Causing anger
D. Causing failure

34. **Where does the author get her definition of "accountability?"**

A. Webster's Dictionary
B. Encyclopedia Britannica
C. Oxford Dictionary
D. World Book Encyclopedia

Mr. Smith gave instructions for the painting to be hung on the wall. And then it leaped forth before his eyes: the little cottages on the river, the white clouds floating over the valley and the green of the towering mountain ranges which were seen in the distance. The painting was so vivid that it seemed almost real. Mr. Smith was now absolutely certain that the painting had been worth money.

35. What does the author mean by the expression "it leaped forth before his eyes"?

A. The painting fell off the wall.
B. The painting appeared so real it was almost three-dimensional.
C. The painting struck Mr. Smith in the face.
D. Mr. Smith was hallucinating.

36. From the last sentence, one can infer that

A. The painting was expensive.
B. The painting was cheap.
C. Mr. Smith was considering purchasing the painting.
D. Mr. Smith thought the painting was too expensive and decided not to purchase it.

37. What is the main idea of this passage?

A. The painting that Mr. Smith purchased is expensive.
B. Mr. Smith purchased a painting.
C. Mr. Smith was pleased with the quality of the painting he had purchased.
D. The painting depicted cottages and valleys.

38. The author's purpose is to

A. Inform
B. Entertain
C. Persuade
D. Narrate

39. What is the meaning of the word "vivid" in the third sentence?

A. Lifelike
B. Dark
C. Expensive
D. Big

40. Is this passage biased?

A. Yes
B. No

Chili peppers may turn out to be the wonder drug of the decade. the fiery fruit comes in many sizes, shapes and colors, all of which grow on plants that are genetic descendants of the tepin plant, originally native to the Americas. Connoisseurs of the regional cuisines of the South west and Louisiana are already well aware that food flavored with chilies can cause a good sweat, but medical researchers are learning more every day about the medical power of capsaicin, the ingredient in the peppers that produces the heat.

Capsaicin as a pain medication has been a part of fold medicine for centuries. It is, in fact, the active ingredient in several currently available over-the-counter liniments for sore muscles. Recent research has been examining the value of the compound for the treatment of other painful conditions. Capsaicin shows some promise in the treatment of phantom limb syndrome, as well as shingles, and some types of headaches. Additional research focuses upon the use of capsaicin to relieve pain in post-surgical patients. Scientists speculate that application of the compound to the skin cause the body to release endorphins – natural pain relievers manufactured by the body itself. An alternative theory holds that capsaicin somehow interferes with t transmission of signals along the nerve fibers, thus reducing the sensation of pain.

In addition to its well-documented history as a pain killer, capsaicin has recently received attention as a phytochemical, one of the naturally occurring compounds from foods that show cancer-fighting qualities. Like the phytochemical sulfoaphane found in broccoli, capsaicin might turn out to be an agent capable of short-circuiting the actions of carcinogens at the cell level before they can cause cancer.

41.   **The author's primary purpose is to:**
A.   entertain the reader with unusual stories about chilies.
B.   narrate the story of the discover of capsaicin.
C.   describe the medicinal properties of the tepin plant.
D.   inform the reader of the medical research about capsaicin.

42.   **All of the following medical problems have been treated using capsaicin EXCEPT:**
A.   cancer.
B.   shingles.
C.   sore muscles.
D.   headache.

43.   **The statement "Chili peppers may turn out to be the wonder drug of the decade," is a statement of:**
A.   fact.
B.   opinion.

On January 24, 1993, retired justice of the Supreme Court Thurgood Marshall, 84, died of heart failure. The media world-wide marked his passing with eulogies, testimonials, remembrances, and biographies. These usually began, "The first Black justice on the Supreme Court," and if this alone were his only accomplishment, it would have earned him a place in history. But his legacy was guaranteed more by his presence in front of the bench than behind it. Thurgood Marshall, attorney-at-law, was creator of the civil rights legislation that took the movement from the marches in the street to the law of the land.

It is easy to see the significance of events in retrospect, difficult while they were occurring. the high school teacher who made Marshall read the Constitution out loud as a punishment could never have foreseen the irony of the act. Marshall's intimate familiarity with the Constitution enabled him to survive the antagonistic nomination hearings in Congress years later. in college, the biology teacher who clashed with Marshall could not have known that by discouraging a would-be dentist, he was creating a dynamic attorney. And likewise, college classmates like Langston Hughes, who would become a writer. Cab Calloway, who would entertain millions, and Nnamdi Azikiew, who would become president of Nigeria, could not know what they started when the goaded their friend to join them in a vote for the integration of their college's faculty.

Marshall graduated from Lincoln College in 1930 and went onto graduate from Howard University's law school. After struggling in a private practice, he was hired as an assistant attorney for the NAACO. In Texas, he obtained protection for black jurors. In Maryland he located a college graduate who had been denied admission into the University of Maryland's all-white law school – as Marshall himself had been denied – and took the university to court. Marshall's eloquence wont he case at the local level even though he anticipated having to take the case to the Supreme Court.

Eventually, Marshall did argue cases in front of the Supreme Court. Many were on the behalf of the NAACP – for whom Marshall won 29 out of 32 cases- and later, under President Lyndon Johnson, Marshall argued as Solicitor General. His legal acumen was responsible for the Supreme Court's decision that made segregation of buses illegal, a precedent that paved the way for the successful Montgomery, Alabama boycott led by Reverend Martin Luther King, Jr. As Solicitor General, Marshall argued the case that resulted in the Miranda rule requiring that suspects be informed of their rights, The most famous case that Marshall argued before the Supreme Court was the landmark "Brown versus Board of Education" which legally ended segregation in schools.

Outspoken and articulate, Thurgood Marshall's work was essentially behind the scenes when contrasted with other leaders in the Civil Rights Movement. But without his expertise and willingness to face prejudice and fear head-on and in the courtroom, the movement could have died. It took the force of law to enable the drive for equality to gain momentum.

45. **The primary organization pattern used in this passage is:**

   A. cause and effect.
   B. order of importance.
   C. summary.
   D. description.

46. **What is the tone of this passage?**

   A. ironic.
   B. reverent.
   C. ambivalent.
   D. indignant.

47. **What is the relationship between the sentence beginning "It is easy to see…" and the sentence beginning "And likewise…?"**

   A. clarification
   B. cause and effect
   C. time order
   D. order of importance

48. **The word acumen most nearly means:**

   A. wittiness.
   B. profession.
   C. expertise.
   D. assistant.

49. **The writer of this passage is probably:**

   A. involved in legal matters of the law.
   B. touched or saddened by Marshall's death.
   C. respectful of the Constitution.
   D. actively interested in politics.

50. **According to the passage, Thurgood Marshall graduated from law school at which college or university.**

   A. Lincoln College
   B. University of Maryland
   C. University of Alabama
   D. Howard University

Answer Key: Reading

1. B.		26. A.	
2. A.		27. B.	
3. C.		28. C.	
4. D.		29. D.	
5. C.		30. A.	
6. B.		31. C.	
7. B.		32. D.	
8. A.		33. A.	
9. B.		34. C.	
10. B.		35. B.	
11. A.		36. A.	
12. D.		37. C.	
13. C.		38. D.	
14. A.		39. A.	
15. D.		40. B.	
16. B.		41. D.	
17. C.		42. A.	
18. C.		43. B.	
19. A.		44. B.	
20. D.		45. C.	
21. A.		46. B.	
22. D.		47. A.	
23. D.		48. C.	
24. D.		49. B.	
25. B.		50. D.	

Answers with Rationale: Reading

1. B. The writer uses expressions such as "protective gear" and "child's protection" to emphasize this.

2. A. The author states that "it seems cruel to expect them to learn as normal children do," thereby indicating that she feels sorry for them.

3. C. The author states that she wonders "why parents subject these children to the pressures of schooling" and that "it seems cruel to expect them to learn as normal children do." In making these statements she appears to be expressing the belief that these children should not have to do what "normal" children do. They have enough to deal with – their illness itself.

4. D. The writer states this fact in the opening sentence.

5. C. The author is simply describing her experience in working with children with cystic fibrosis.

6. B. The author mentions tutoring children with cystic fibrosis in her opening sentence and goes on to "explain" some of these issues that are involved with her job.

7. B. The fact that she states that it "seems" cruel indicates there is no evidence to support this belief.

8. A. The writer clearly feels sorry for these children and gears her writing in that direction.

9. B. In mentioning the their life expectancies are short, she is explaining by giving one reason why it is cruel to expect them to learn as normal children do.

10. B. Even though to most readers, the writer's argument makes good sense, it is biased and lacks real evidence.

11. A. Any of the other choices would be redundant in this sentence.

12. D. The author simply states the types of disciplinary styles.

13. C. This is directly stated in the second paragraph.

14. A. Choice C is not true, the opposite is stated in the passage. Choice B could be true, but we have no evidence of this. Choice D is just one of the many facts listed in the passage.

15. D. The author is providing the reader with information about disciplinary practices.

16. B. If the reader were so inclined, he could research discipline and find this information.

17. C. The author appears to simply be stating the facts.

18. C. The author has taken a subject, in this case discipline, and developed it point by point.

19. A. The author appears to have done extensive research on this subject.

20. D. Given all the facts mentioned in the passage, this is the only inference one can make.

21. A. This fact is directly stated in the second paragraph.

22. D. The meaning of this word is directly stated in the same sentence.

23. D. The author goes on to further explain what she meant by"...what exactly does that mean?" in the first paragraph.

24. D. Most of the passage is dedicated to elaborating on why teacher assessment is such a problem.

25. B. In the third paragraph, the author appears to be resentful of lazy teachers.

26. A. The first sentence of the third paragraph alludes to this.

27. B. There may be those who feel they can be good teachers by using old methods.

28. C. This fact is directly stated in the first paragraph.

29. D. The author does some describing, but the majority of her statements seemed geared towards convincing the reader that teachers who are lazy or who do not keep current should be fired.

30. A. The entire third paragraph is the author's opinion on the matter.

31. C. The author identifies teacher assessment as a problem and spends the rest of the passage defining why it is considered a problem.

32. D. The author appears concerned with the future of education.

33. A. The first paragraph makes this definition clear.

34. C. This is directly stated in the third sentence of the first paragraph.

35. B. This is almost directly stated in the third sentence.

36. A. Choice B is incorrect because, had the painting been cheap, chances are that Mr. Smith would no have considered his purchase. Choices C and D are ruled out by the fact that the painting had already been purchased. The author makes this clear when she says, "...the painting had been worth the money."

37. C. Every sentence in the paragraph alludes to this fact.

38. D. The author is simply narrating or telling the story of Mr. Smith and his painting.

39. A. This is reinforced by the second half of the same sentence.

40. B. The author appears to just be telling what happened when Mr. Smith had his new painting hung on the wall.

41. D. This purpose is conveyed in the last sentence of paragraph one.

42. A. is the exception. The passage states that capsaicin "might turn out to be" effective in fighting cancer, but actual cancer treatments with the drug are not mentioned.

43. B. The statement reflects a probability – a prediction of a future occurrence – which cannot be verified.

44. B. Endorphins are defined; the context clue is the punctuation (dashes) which sets off the definition.

45. C. Overall the passage summarizes Marshall's life and what was written about him when he died. The other choices for this question are somewhat appealing, and may have some basis in the text. However, attention must be directed and the primary pattern of organization.

46. B. The passage uniformly conveys a sense of awe, respect, and wonder towards Marshall and his accomplishments. Marshall is said to have "a place in history" and his contribution to the Civil Rights Movement is glowingly described in the last paragraph.

47. A. The second sentence restates in more specific terms the general idea stated in the first sentence.

48. C. This choice indicates a combination of knowledge and experience.

49. B. This passage is a eulogy, which offers praise in honor of one who has died.

50. D. Howard University is mentioned in paragraph three.

COMPETENCY 7.0 USE NUMBER CONCEPTS AND COMPUTATION SKILLS

Skill 7.1   Add, subtract, multiply, divide fractions, decimals, and integers.

Rational numbers can be expressed as the ratio of two integers, $\frac{a}{b}$ where $b \neq 0$, for example $\frac{2}{3}$, $-\frac{4}{5}$, $5 = \frac{5}{1}$.

The rational numbers include integers, fractions and mixed numbers, terminating and repeating decimals. Every rational number can be expressed as a repeating or terminating decimal and can be shown on a number line.

Integers are positive and negative whole numbers and zero.
    ...-6, -5, -4, -3, -2, -1, 0, 1, 2, 3, 4, 5, 6, ...

Whole numbers are natural numbers and zero.
    0, 1, 2, 3, ,4 ,5 ,6 ...

Natural numbers are the counting numbers.
    1, 2, 3, 4, 5, 6, ...

Irrational numbers are real numbers that cannot be written as the ratio of two integers. These are infinite non-repeating decimals.
    <u>Examples</u>: $\sqrt{5}$ = 2.2360.., pi =∏ = 3.1415927...

A **fraction** is an expression of numbers in the form of x/y, where x is the numerator and y is the denominator, which cannot be zero.

Example: $\dfrac{3}{7}$ 3 is the numerator; 7 is the denominator

If the fraction has common factors for the numerator and denominator, divide both by the common factor to reduce the fraction to its lowest form.

Example:

$$\frac{13}{39} = \frac{1 \times 13}{3 \times 13} = \frac{1}{3}$$ Divide by the common factor 13

A **mixed** number has an integer part and a fractional part.

Example: $2\dfrac{1}{4}$, $^{-}5\dfrac{1}{6}$, $7\dfrac{1}{3}$

Percent = per 100 (written with the symbol %). Thus $10\% = \dfrac{10}{100} = \dfrac{1}{10}$.

Decimals = deci = part of ten. To find the decimal equivalent of a fraction, use the denominator to divide the numerator as shown in the following example.

Example: Find the decimal equivalent of $\dfrac{7}{10}$.

Since 10 cannot divide into 7 evenly

$$\dfrac{7}{10} = 0.7$$

Properties are rules that apply for addition, subtraction, multiplication, or division of real numbers. These properties are:

Commutative: You can change the order of the terms or factors as follows.

For addition: $a + b = b + a$
For multiplication: $ab = ba$

Since addition is the inverse operation of subtraction and multiplication is the inverse operation of division, no separate laws are needed for subtraction and division.

Example: $5 + {}^-8 = {}^-8 + 5 = {}^-3$

Example: $^-2 \times 6 = 6 \times {}^-2 = {}^-12$

Associative: You can regroup the terms as you like.

For addition: $a + (b + c) = (a + b) + c$
For multiplication: $a(bc) = (ab)c$

This rule does not apply for division and subtraction.

Example: $({}^-2 + 7) + 5 = {}^-2 + (7 + 5)$
$5 + 5 = {}^-2 + 12 = 10$

Example: $(3 \times {}^-7) \times 5 = 3 \times ({}^-7 \times 5)$
$^-21 \times 5 = 3 \times {}^-35 = {}^-105$

Identity: Finding a number so that when added to a term results in that number (additive identity); finding a number such that when multiplied by a term results in that number (multiplicative identity).

For addition: $a + 0 = a$ (zero is additive identity)
For multiplication: $a \cdot 1 = a$ (one is multiplicative)

Example: $17 + 0 = 17$

Example: $^-34 \times 1 = {}^-34$
The product of any number and one is that number.

Inverse: Finding a number such that when added to the number it results in zero; or when multiplied by the number results in 1.

For addition: $a + (-a) = 0$
For multiplication: $a \cdot (1/a) = 1$

($-a$) is the additive inverse of a; ($1/a$), also called the reciprocal, is the multiplicative inverse of a.

Example: $25 + {}^-25 = 0$

Example: $5 \times \frac{1}{5} = 1$ The product of any number and its reciprocal is one.

Distributive: This technique allows us to operate on terms within a parentheses without first performing operations within the parentheses. This is especially helpful when terms within the parentheses cannot be combined.

$a\,(b + c) = ab + ac$

Example: $6 \times ({}^-4 + 9) = (6 \times {}^-4) + (6 \times 9)$
   $6 \times 5 = {}^-24 + 54 = 30$

To multiply a sum by a number, multiply each addend by the number, then add the products.

Addition of whole numbers

Example: At the end of a day of shopping, a shopper had $24 remaining in his wallet. He spent $45 on various goods. How much money did the shopper have at the beginning of the day?

The total amount of money the shopper started with is the sum of the amount spent and the amount remaining at the end of the day.

$$\begin{array}{r} 24 \\ +\ \ 45 \\ \hline 69 \end{array}$$ → The original total was $69.

Example: A race took the winner 1 hr. 58 min. 12 sec. on the first half of the race and 2 hr. 9 min. 57 sec. on the second half of the race. How much time did the entire race take?

$$\begin{array}{l} \quad 1 \text{ hr. } 58 \text{ min. } 12 \text{ sec.} \\ +\ 2 \text{ hr. } \ 9 \text{ min. } 57 \text{ sec.} \quad \text{Add these numbers} \\ \hline \quad \ 3 \text{ hr. } 67 \text{ min. } 69 \text{ sec.} \\ +\ 1 \text{ min -60 sec.} \qquad \text{Change 60 seconds to 1} \\ \hline \qquad\qquad\qquad\qquad\quad \text{min.} \\ \quad \ 3 \text{ hr. } 68 \text{ min. } \ 9 \text{ sec.} \\ +\ 1 \text{ hr.-60 min.} \qquad \text{Change 60 minutes to 1 hr.} \\ \hline \quad \ 4 \text{ hr. } \ 8 \text{ min. } \ 9 \text{ sec.} \ \leftarrow \text{final answer} \end{array}$$

Subtraction of Whole Numbers

Example: At the end of his shift, a cashier has $96 in the cash register. At the beginning of his shift, he had $15. How much money did the cashier collect during his shift?

The total collected is the difference of the ending amount and the starting amount.

$$\begin{array}{r} 96 \\ -\ \ 15 \\ \hline 81 \end{array}$$ → The total collected was $81.

Multiplication of whole numbers

Multiplication is one of the four basic number operations. In simple terms, multiplication is the addition of a number to itself a certain number of times. For example, 4 multiplied by 3 is the equal to 4 + 4 + 4 or 3 + 3 + 3 +3. Another way of conceptualizing multiplication is to think in terms of groups. For example, if we have 4 groups of 3 students, the total number of students is 4 multiplied by 3. We call the solution to a multiplication problem the product.

The basic algorithm for whole number multiplication begins with aligning the numbers by place value with the number containing more places on top.

$$172$$
$$\underline{x \quad 43} \longrightarrow$$ Note that we placed 122 on top because it has more places than 43 does.

Next, we multiply the ones' place of the second number by each place value of the top number sequentially.

$$(2)$$
$$172$$
$$\underline{x \quad 43} \longrightarrow$$
$$516$$

{3 x 2 = 6, 3 x 7 = 21, 3 x 1 = 3}
Note that we had to carry a 2 to the hundreds' column because 3 x 7 = 21. Note also that we add, not multiply, carried numbers to the product.

Next, we multiply the number in the tens' place of the second number by each place value of the top number sequentially. Because we are multiplying by a number in the tens' place, we place a zero at the end of this product.

$$(2)$$
$$172$$
$$\underline{x \quad 43} \longrightarrow$$
$$516$$
$$6880$$

{4 x 2 = 8, 4 x 7 = 28, 4 x 1 = 4}

Finally, to determine the final product we add the two partial products.

$$172$$
$$\underline{x \quad 43}$$
$$516$$
$$\underline{+ \; 6880}$$
$$7396 \longrightarrow$$ The product of 172 and 43 is 7396.

Example: A student buys 4 boxes of crayons. Each box contains 16 crayons. How many total crayons does the student have?

The total number of crayons is 16 x 4.

$$\begin{array}{r} 16 \\ \times\ 4 \\ \hline 64 \end{array}$$ ⟶ Total number of crayons equals 64.

Division of whole numbers

Division, the inverse of multiplication, is another of the four basic number operations. When we divide one number by another, we determine how many times we can multiply the divisor (number divided by) before we exceed the number we are dividing (dividend). For example, 8 divided by 2 equals 4 because we can multiply 2 four times to reach 8 (2 x 4 = 8 or 2 + 2 + 2 + 2 = 8). Using the grouping conceptualization we used with multiplication, we can divide 8 into 4 groups of 2 or 2 groups of 4. We call the answer to a division problem the quotient.

If the divisor does not divide evenly into the dividend, we express the leftover amount either as a remainder or as a fraction with the divisor as the denominator. For example, 9 divided by 2 equals 4 with a remainder of 1 or 4 ½.

The basic algorithm for division is long division. We start by representing the quotient as follows.

$14\overline{)293}$ ⟶ 14 is the divisor and 293 is the dividend.

This represents 293 ÷ 14.

Next, we divide the divisor into the dividend starting from the left.

$14\overline{)293}$ with 2 above ⟶ 14 divides into 29 two times with a remainder.

Next, we multiply the partial quotient by the divisor, subtract this value from the first digits of the dividend, and bring down the remaining dividend digits to complete the number.

$\begin{array}{r} 2 \\ 14\overline{)293} \\ -28 \\ \hline 13 \end{array}$ ⟶ 2 x 14 = 28, 29 – 28 = 1, and bringing down the 3 yields 13.

Finally, we divide again (the divisor into the remaining value) and repeat the preceding process. The number left after the subtraction represents the remainder.

$$
\begin{array}{r}
20 \\
14\overline{)293} \\
-28 \\
\hline
13 \\
-0 \\
\hline
13 \\
\end{array}
$$

→ The final quotient is 20 with a remainder of 13. We can also represent this quotient as 20 13/14.

Example: Each box of apples contains 24 apples. How many boxes must a grocer purchase to supply a group of 252 people with one apple each?

The grocer needs 252 apples. Because he must buy apples in groups of 24, we divide 252 by 24 to determine how many boxes he needs to buy.

$$
\begin{array}{r}
10 \\
24\overline{)252} \\
-24 \\
\hline
2 \\
-0 \\
\hline
12 \\
\end{array}
$$

→ The quotient is 10 with a remainder of 12.

Thus, the grocer needs 10 boxes plus 12 more apples. Therefore, the minimum number of boxes the grocer can purchase is 11.

Example: At his job, John gets paid $20 for every hour he works. If John made $940 in a week, how many hours did he work?

This is a division problem. To determine the number of hours John worked, we divide the total amount made ($940) by the hourly rate of pay ($20). Thus, the number of hours worked equals 940 divided by 20.

$$
\begin{array}{r}
47 \\
20\overline{)940} \\
-80 \\
\hline
140 \\
-140 \\
\hline
0 \\
\end{array}
$$

→ 20 divides into 940, 47 times with no remainder.

John worked 47 hours.

Addition and Subtraction of Decimals

When adding and subtracting decimals, we align the numbers by place value as we do with whole numbers. After adding or subtracting each column, we bring the decimal down, placing it in the same location as in the numbers added or subtracted.

Example: Find the sum of 152.3 and 36.342.

```
    152.300
+    36.342
    188.642
```

Note that we placed two zeroes after the final place value in 152.3 to clarify the column addition.

Example: Find the difference of 152.3 and 36.342.

```
      2 9 10                  (4)11(12)
    152.300          152.300
-    36.342    →    -    36.342
        58              115.958
```

Note how we borrowed to subtract from the zeroes in the hundredths' and thousandths' place of 152.300.

Multiplication of Decimals

When multiplying decimal numbers, we multiply exactly as with whole numbers and place the decimal moving in from the left the total number of decimal places contained in the two numbers multiplied. For example, when multiplying 1.5 and 2.35, we place the decimal in the product 3 places in from the left (3.525).

Example: Find the product of 3.52 and 4.1.

```
     3.52  ———→   Note that there are 3 total decimal places
   x  4.1         in the two numbers.
     352
+  14080  ———→
   14432          We place the decimal 3 places in from the
                  left.
```

Thus, the final product is 14.432.

Example: A shopper has 5 one-dollar bills, 6 quarters, 3 nickels, and 4 pennies in his pocket. How much money does he have?

$$3$$

5 x $1.00 = $5.00	$0.25	$0.05	$0.01
	x 6	x 3	x 4
	$1.50	$0.15	$0.04

Note the placement of the decimals in the multiplication products. Thus, the total amount of money in the shopper's pocket is:

$$\begin{array}{r} \$5.00 \\ 1.50 \\ 0.15 \\ +\ 0.04 \\ \hline \$6.69 \end{array}$$

Division of Decimals

When dividing decimal numbers, we first remove the decimal in the divisor by moving the decimal in the dividend the same number of spaces to the right. For example, when dividing 1.45 into 5.3 we convert the numbers to 145 and 530 and perform normal whole number division.

Example: Find the quotient of 5.3 divided by 1.45.
            Convert to 145 and 530.

Divide.

$$\begin{array}{r} 3 \\ 145)\overline{530} \\ -\ 435 \\ \hline 95 \end{array} \longrightarrow \begin{array}{r} 3.65 \\ 145)\overline{530.00} \\ -\ 435 \\ \hline 950 \\ -\ 870 \\ \hline 800 \end{array} \longrightarrow$$

Note that we insert the decimal to continue division.

Because one of the numbers divided contained one decimal place, we round the quotient to one decimal place. Thus, the final quotient is 3.7.

Addition and subtraction of fractions

<u>Key Points</u>

1.   You need a common denominator in order to add and subtract reduced and improper fractions.

Example: $\dfrac{1}{3} + \dfrac{7}{3} = \dfrac{1+7}{3} = \dfrac{8}{3} = 2\dfrac{2}{3}$

Example: $\dfrac{4}{12} + \dfrac{6}{12} - \dfrac{3}{12} = \dfrac{4+6-3}{12} = \dfrac{7}{12}$

2.   Adding an integer and a fraction of the <u>same</u> sign results directly in a mixed fraction.

Example: $2 + \dfrac{2}{3} = 2\dfrac{2}{3}$

Example: $^{-}2 - \dfrac{3}{4} = {}^{-}2\dfrac{3}{4}$

3.   Adding an integer and a fraction with different signs involves the following steps.

-get a common denominator
-add or subtract as needed
-change to a mixed fraction if possible

Example: $2 - \dfrac{1}{3} = \dfrac{2 \times 3 - 1}{3} = \dfrac{6-1}{3} = \dfrac{5}{3} = 1\dfrac{2}{3}$

Example: Add $7\dfrac{3}{8} + 5\dfrac{2}{7}$

Add the whole numbers; add the fractions and combine the two results:

$7\dfrac{3}{8} + 5\dfrac{2}{7} = (7+5) + (\dfrac{3}{8} + \dfrac{2}{7})$

$= 12 + \dfrac{(7 \times 3) + (8 \times 2)}{56}$ (LCM of 8 and 7)

$= 12 + \dfrac{21+16}{56} = 12 + \dfrac{37}{56} = 12\dfrac{37}{56}$

Example: Perform the operation.

$$\frac{2}{3} - \frac{5}{6}$$

We first find the LCM of 3 and 6 which is 6.

$$\frac{2 \times 2}{3 \times 2} - \frac{5}{6} \rightarrow \frac{4-5}{6} = \frac{^-1}{6}$$ (Using method A)

Example: $^-7\frac{1}{4} + 2\frac{7}{8}$

$$^-7\frac{1}{4} + 2\frac{7}{8} = (^-7+2) + (\frac{^-1}{4} + \frac{7}{8})$$

$$= (^-5) + \frac{(^-2+7)}{8} = (^-5) + (\frac{5}{8})$$

$$= (^-5) + \frac{5}{8} = \frac{^-5 \times 8}{1 \times 8} + \frac{5}{8} = \frac{^-40+5}{8}$$

$$= \frac{^-35}{8} = ^-4\frac{3}{8}$$

Divide 35 by 8 to get 4, remainder 3.

Caution: Common error would be

$$^-7\frac{1}{4} + 2\frac{7}{8} = ^-7\frac{2}{8} + 2\frac{7}{8} = ^-5\frac{9}{8}$$ Wrong.

It is correct to add -7 and 2 to get -5, but adding $\frac{2}{8} + \frac{7}{8} = \frac{9}{8}$

is wrong. It should have been $\frac{^-2}{8} + \frac{7}{8} = \frac{5}{8}$. Then,

$$^-5 + \frac{5}{8} = ^-4\frac{3}{8}$$ as before.

Multiplication of fractions

Using the following example: $3\frac{1}{4} \times \frac{5}{6}$

1. Convert each number to an improper fraction.

$$3\frac{1}{4} = \frac{(12+1)}{4} = \frac{13}{4} \qquad\qquad \frac{5}{6} \text{ is already in reduced form.}$$

2. Reduce (cancel) common factors of the numerator and denominator if they exist.

$$\frac{13}{4} \times \frac{5}{6} \qquad \text{No common factors exist.}$$

3. Multiply the numerators by each other and the denominators by each other.

$$\frac{13}{4} \times \frac{5}{6} = \frac{65}{24}$$

4. If possible, reduce the fraction back to its lowest term.

$$\frac{65}{24} \quad \text{Cannot be reduced further.}$$

5. Convert the improper fraction back to a mixed fraction by using long division.

$$\frac{65}{24} = 24\overline{)65} \qquad = 2\frac{17}{24}$$
$$\phantom{\frac{65}{24} = 24\overline{)}}\underline{48}$$
$$\phantom{\frac{65}{24} = 24\overline{)}6}17$$

Summary of sign changes for multiplication:

a. $(+) \times (+) = (+)$

b. $(-) \times (+) = (-)$

c. $(+) \times (-) = (-)$

d. $(-) \times (-) = (+)$

Example: $7\dfrac{1}{3}\times\dfrac{5}{11}=\dfrac{22}{3}\times\dfrac{5}{11}$ Reduce like terms (22 and 11)

$$=\dfrac{2}{3}\times\dfrac{5}{1}=\dfrac{10}{3}=3\dfrac{1}{3}$$

Example: $^{-}6\dfrac{1}{4}\times\dfrac{5}{9}=\dfrac{^{-}25}{4}\times\dfrac{5}{9}$

$$=\dfrac{^{-}125}{36}=^{-}3\dfrac{17}{36}$$

Example: $\dfrac{^{-}1}{4}\times\dfrac{^{-}3}{7}$ Negative times a negative equals positive.

$$=\dfrac{1}{4}\times\dfrac{3}{7}=\dfrac{3}{28}$$

Division of fractions:

1. Change mixed fractions to improper fraction.

2. Change the division problem to a multiplication problem by using the reciprocal of the number after the division sign.

3. Find the sign of the final product.

4. Cancel if common factors exist between the numerator and the denominator.

5. Multiply the numerators together and the denominators together.

6. Change the improper fraction to a mixed number.

Example: $3\dfrac{1}{5}\div 2\dfrac{1}{4}=\dfrac{16}{5}\div\dfrac{9}{4}$

$$=\dfrac{16}{5}\times\dfrac{4}{9}$$ Reciprocal of $\dfrac{9}{4}$ is $\dfrac{4}{9}$.

$$=\dfrac{64}{45}=1\dfrac{19}{45}$$

Example: $\quad 7\dfrac{3}{4} \div 11\dfrac{5}{8} = \dfrac{31}{4} \div \dfrac{93}{8}$

$= \dfrac{31}{4} \times \dfrac{8}{93}$ Reduce like terms.

$= \dfrac{1}{1} \times \dfrac{2}{3} = \dfrac{2}{3}$

Example: $\quad \left(-2\dfrac{1}{2}\right) \div 4\dfrac{1}{6} = \dfrac{^-5}{2} \div \dfrac{25}{6}$

$= \dfrac{^-5}{2} \times \dfrac{6}{25}$ Reduce like terms.

$= \dfrac{^-1}{1} \times \dfrac{3}{5} = \dfrac{^-3}{5}$

Example: $\quad \left(-5\dfrac{3}{8}\right) \div \left(\dfrac{^-7}{16}\right) = \dfrac{^-43}{8} \div \dfrac{^-7}{16}$

$= \dfrac{^-43}{8} \times \dfrac{^-16}{7}$ Reduce like terms.

$= \dfrac{43}{1} \times \dfrac{2}{7}$ Negative times a negative equals a positive.

$= \dfrac{86}{7} = 12\dfrac{2}{7}$

Skill 7.2   Use the order of operations to solve problems.

The Order of Operations are to be followed when evaluating algebraic expressions. Follow these steps in order:

1. Simplify inside grouping characters such as parentheses, brackets, square root, fraction bar, etc.

2. Multiply out expressions with exponents.

3. Do multiplication or division, from left to right.

4. Do addition or subtraction, from left to right.

Example: $3^3 - 5(b + 2)$

$$= 3^3 - 5b - 10$$

$$= 27 - 5b - 10 = 17 - 5b$$

Example: $2 - 4 \times 2^3 - 2(4 - 2 \times 3)$

$$= 2 - 4 \times 2^3 - 2(4 - 6) = 2 - 4 \times 2^3 - 2(^-2)$$

$$= 2 - 4 \times 2^3 + 4 = 2 - 4 \times 8 + 4$$

$$= 2 - 32 + 4 = 6 - 32 = ^- 26$$

Skill 7.3   **Solve problems involving percents.**

Example: 5 is what percent of 20?

This is the same as converting $\dfrac{5}{20}$ to % form.

$$\frac{5}{20} \times \frac{100}{1} = \frac{5}{1} \times \frac{5}{1} = 25\%$$

Example: There are 64 dogs in the kennel. 48 are collies. What percent are collies?

Restate the problem.	48 is what percent of 64?
Write an equation.	$48 = n \times 64$
Solve.	$\frac{48}{64} = n$

$n = \frac{3}{4} = 75\%$

75% of the dogs are collies.

Example: The auditorium was filled to 90% capacity. There were 558 seats occupied. What is the capacity of the auditorium?

Restate the problem.	90% of what number is 558?
Write an equation.	$0.9n = 558$
Solve.	$n = \frac{558}{.9}$
	$n = 620$

The capacity of the auditorium is 620 people.

Example: A pair of shoes costs $42.00. Sales tax is 6%. What is the total cost of the shoes?

Restate the problem.	What is 6% of 42?
Write an equation.	$n = 0.06 \times 42$
Solve.	$n = 2.52$

Add the sales tax to the cost. $42.00 + $2.52 = $44.52

The total cost of the shoes, including sales tax, is $44.52.

Skill 7.4   Perform calculations using exponents and scientific notation.

The **exponent form** is a shortcut method to write repeated multiplication. Basic form: b^n, where b is called the base and n is the exponent. b and n are both real numbers. b^n implies that the base b is multiplied by itself n times.

Examples: $3^4 = 3 \times 3 \times 3 \times 3 = 81$

$2^3 = 2 \times 2 \times 2 = 8$

$(^-2)^4 = (^-2) \times (^-2) \times (^-2) \times (^-2) = 16$

$^-2^4 = {}^- (2 \times 2 \times 2 \times 2) = {}^- 16$

Key exponent rules:

For 'a' nonzero, and 'm' and 'n' real numbers:

1) $a^m \cdot a^n = a^{(m+n)}$ Product rule

2) $\dfrac{a^m}{a^n} = a^{(m-n)}$ Quotient rule

3) $\dfrac{a^{-m}}{a^{-n}} = \dfrac{a^n}{a^m}$

When 10 is raised to any power, the exponent tells the numbers of zeroes in the product.

Example: $10^7 = 10,000,000$

Caution: Unless the negative sign is inside the parentheses and the exponent is outside the parentheses, the sign is not affected by the exponent.

$(^-2)^4$ implies that -2 is multiplied by itself 4 times.

$^-2^4$ implies that 2 is multiplied by itself 4 times, then the answer is negated.

Scientific notation is a more convenient method for writing very large and very small numbers. It employs two factors. The first factor is a number between 1 and 10. The second factor is a power of 10. This notation is a "shorthand" for expressing large numbers (like the weight of 100 elephants) or small numbers (like the weight of an atom in pounds).

Recall that:

$10^n = (10)^n$ Ten multiplied by itself n times.

$10^0 = 1$ Any nonzero number raised to power of zero is 1.

$10^1 = 10$

$10^2 = 10 \times 10 = 100$

$10^3 = 10 \times 10 \times 10 = 1000$ (kilo)

$10^{-1} = 1/10$ (deci)

$10^{-2} = 1/100$ (centi)

$10^{-3} = 1/1000$ (milli)

$10^{-6} = 1/1,000,000$ (micro)

Example: Write 46,368,000 in scientific notation.

    1)   Introduce a decimal point and decimal places.
46,368,000 = 46,368,000.0000

    2)   Make a mark between the two digits that give a number between -9.9 and 9.9.
4 ∧ 6,368,000 .0000

    3)   Count the number of digit places between the decimal point and the ∧ mark. This number is the 'n'-the power of ten.

So, $46,368,000 = 4.6368 \times 10^7$

Example: Write 0.00397 in scientific notation.

    1)   Decimal place is already in place.

    2)   Make a mark between 3 and 9 to get a one number between -9.9 and 9.9.

    3)   Move decimal place to the mark (3 hops).

0.003 ∧ 97

Motion is to the right, so n of 10^n is negative.

Therefore, $0.00397 = 3.97 \times 10^{-3}$.

Skill 7.5   Estimate solutions to problems.

To estimate measurement of familiar objects, it is first necessary to determine the units to be used.

Examples:
Length
1. The coastline of Florida
2. The width of a ribbon
3. The thickness of a book
4. The depth of water in a pool

Weight or mass
1. A bag of sugar
2. A school bus
3. A dime

Capacity or volume
1. Paint to paint a bedroom
2. Glass of milk

Money
1. Cost of a house
2. Cost of a cup of coffee
3. Exchange rate

Perimeter
1. The edge of a backyard
2. The edge of a football field

Area
1. The size of a carpet
2. The size of a state

Example: Estimate the measurements of the following objects:

Length of a dollar bill	6 inches
Weight of a baseball	1 pound
Distance from New York to Florida	1100 km
Volume of water to fill a medicine dropper	1 milliliter
Length of a desk	2 meters
Temperature of water in a swimming pool	80 ° F

Depending on the degree of accuracy needed, an object may be measured to different units. For example, a pencil may be 6 inches to the nearest inch, or 6 3 8 inches to the
nearest eighth of an inch. Similarly, it might be 15 cm to the nearest cm or 154 mm to the nearest mm.

Given a set of objects and their measurements, the use of rounding procedures is helpful when attempting to round to the nearest given unit. When rounding to a given place value, it is necessary to look at the number in the next smaller place. If this number is 5 or more, the number in the place we are rounding to is increased by one and all numbers to the right are changed to zero. If the number is less than 5, the number in the place we are rounding to stays the same and all numbers to the right are changed to zero.

One method of rounding measurements can require an additional step. First, the measurement must be converted to a decimal number. Then the rules for rounding applied.

Example: Round the measurements to the given units.

MEASUREMENT	ROUND TO NEAREST	ANSWER
1 foot 7 inches	foot	2 ft
5 pound 6 ounces	pound	5 pounds
5 9/16 inches	inch	6 inches

Convert each measurement to a decimal number. Then apply the rules for rounding.

1 foot 7 inches = $1\frac{7}{12}$ ft = 1.58333 ft, round up to 2 ft

5 pounds 6 ounces = $5\frac{6}{16}$ pounds = 5.375 pound, round to 5 pounds

$5\frac{9}{16}$ inches = 5.5625 inches, round up to 6 inches

Example: Janet goes into a store to purchase a CD on sale for $13.95. While shopping, she sees two pairs of shoes, prices $19.95 and $14.50. She only has $50. Can she purchase everything?

Solve by rounding:

$19.95→$20.00
$14.50→$15.00
$13.95→$14.00
$49.00   Yes, she can purchase the CD and the shoes.

Skill 7.6 **Use the concepts of "less than" and "greater than."**

Symbol for inequality: In the symbol ' $>$ ' (greater than) or ' $<$ ' (less than), the big open side of the symbol always faces the larger of the two numbers and the point of the symbol always faces the smaller number.

Example: Compare 15 and 20 on the number line.

Since 20 is further away from the zero than 15 is, then 20 is greater than 15, or $20 > 15$.

Example: Compare $\dfrac{3}{7}$ and $\dfrac{5}{10}$.

To compare fractions, they should have the same least common denominator (LCD). The LCD in this example is 70.

$$\frac{3}{7} = \frac{3 \times 10}{7 \times 10} = \frac{30}{70} \qquad\qquad \frac{5}{10} = \frac{5 \times 7}{10 \times 7} = \frac{35}{70}$$

Since the denominators are equal, compare only the denominators. $30 < 35$, so:

$$\frac{3}{7} < \frac{5}{10}$$

COMPETENCY 8.0 SOLVE WORD PROBLEMS INVOLVING INTEGERS, FRACTIONS, OR DECIMALS

Skill 8.1 **Solve word problems involving integers, fractions, decimals, and percents**

See Competency 7.0.

Skill 8.2 **Solve word problems involving ratios, and proportions**

A **ratio** is a comparison of 2 numbers. If a class had 11 boys and 14 girls, the ratio of boys to girls could be written one of 3 ways:

$$11:14 \quad \text{or} \quad 11 \text{ to } 14 \quad \text{or} \quad \frac{11}{14}$$

The ratio of girls to boys is:

$$14:11, \ 14 \text{ to } 11 \text{ or } \frac{14}{11}$$

Ratios can be reduced when possible. A ratio of 12 cats to 18 dogs would reduce to 2:3, 2 to 3 or $2/3$.

Note: Read ratio questions carefully. Given a group of 6 adults and 5 children, the ratio of children to the entire group would be 5:11.

A **proportion** is an equation in which a fraction is set equal to another. To solve the proportion, multiply each numerator times the other fraction's denominator. Set these two products equal to each other and solve the resulting equation. This is called **cross-multiplying** the proportion.

Example: $\frac{4}{15} = \frac{x}{60}$ is a proportion.

To solve this, cross multiply.

$(4)(60) = (15)(x)$

$240 = 15x$

$16 = x$

Example: $\dfrac{x+3}{3x+4} = \dfrac{2}{5}$ is a proportion.

To solve, cross multiply.

$5(x+3) = 2(3x+4)$

$5x+15 = 6x+8$

$7 = x$

Example: $\dfrac{x+2}{8} = \dfrac{2}{x-4}$ is another proportion.

To solve, cross multiply.

$(x+2)(x-4) = 8(2)$

$x^2 - 2x - 8 = 16$

$x^2 - 2x - 24 = 0$

$(x-6)(x+4) = 0$

$x = 6$ or $x = {}^-4$

Proportions can be used to solve word problems whenever relationships are compared. Some situations include scale drawings and maps, similar polygons, speed, time and distance, cost, and comparison shopping.

Example 1:   Which is the better buy, 6 items for $1.29 or 8 items for $1.69?

Find the unit price.

$\dfrac{6}{1.29} = \dfrac{1}{x}$ $\dfrac{8}{1.69} = \dfrac{1}{x}$

$6x = 1.29$ $8x = 1.69$

$x = 0.215$ $x = 0.21125$

Thus, 6 items for $1.29 is the better buy.

Example: A car travels 125 miles in 2.5 hours.. How far will it go in 6 hours?

Write a proportion comparing the distance and time.

$\dfrac{miles}{hours}$ $\dfrac{125}{2.5} = \dfrac{x}{6}$

$2.5x = 750$

$x = 300$

Thus, the car can travel 300 miles in 6 hours.

Example: The scale on a map is $\frac{3}{4}$ inch = 6 miles. What is the actual distance between two cities if they are $1\frac{1}{2}$ inches apart on the map?

Write a proportion comparing the scale to the actual distance.

scale   actual

$$\frac{\frac{3}{4}}{1\frac{1}{2}} = \frac{6}{x}$$

$$\frac{3}{4}x = 1\frac{1}{2} \times 6$$

$$\frac{3}{4}x = 9$$

$$x = 12$$

Thus, the actual distance between the cities is 12 miles.

COMPETENCY 9.0 INTERPRET INFORMATION FROM A GRAPH, TABLE OR CHART

Skill 9.1   **Interpret information in line graphs, bar graphs, pie graphs, pictographs, tables, charts, or graphs of functions.**

To make a **bar graph** or a **pictograph**, determine the scale to be used for the graph. Then determine the length of each bar on the graph or determine the number of pictures needed to represent each item of information. Be sure to include an explanation of the scale in the legend.

Example: A class had the following grades:
4 A's, 9 B's, 8 C's, 1 D, 3 F's.
Graph these on a bar graph and a pictograph.

Pictograph

Grade	Number of Students
A	☺☺☺☺
B	☺☺☺☺☺☺☺☺☺
C	☺☺☺☺☺☺☺☺
D	☺
F	☺☺☺

Bar graph

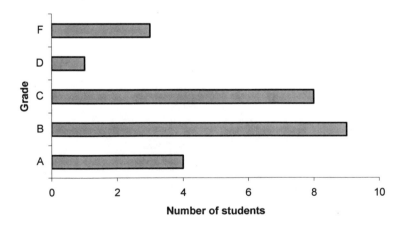

To make a **line graph**, determine appropriate scales for both the vertical and horizontal axes (based on the information to be graphed). Describe what each axis represents and mark the scale periodically on each axis. Graph the individual points of the graph and connect the points on the graph from left to right.

Example: Graph the following information using a line graph.

The number of National Merit finalists/school year

	90-91	91-92	92-93	93-94	94-95	95-96
Central	3	5	1	4	6	8
Wilson	4	2	3	2	3	2

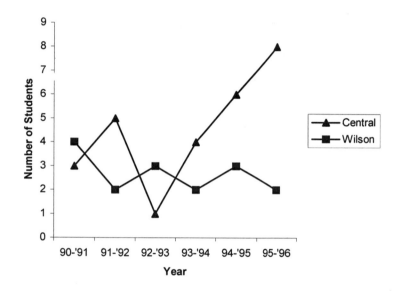

To make a **circle graph**, total all the information that is to be included on the graph. Determine the central angle to be used for each sector of the graph using the following formula:

$$\frac{\text{information}}{\text{total information}} \times 360° = \text{degrees in central} \measuredangle$$

Lay out the central angles to these sizes, label each section and include its percent.

Example: Graph this information on a circle graph:

Monthly expenses:

Rent, $400
Food, $150
Utilities, $75
Clothes, $75
Church, $100
Misc., $200

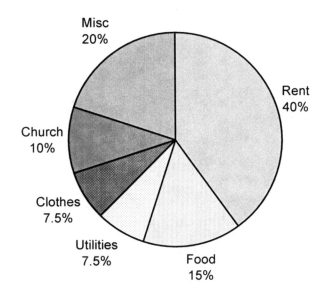

Scatter plots compare two characteristics of the same group of things or people and usually consist of a large body of data. They show how much one variable is affected by another. The relationship between the two variables is their **correlation**. The closer the data points come to making a straight line when plotted, the closer the correlation.

Stem and leaf plots are visually similar to line plots. The **stems** are the digits in the greatest place value of the data values, and the **leaves** are the digits in the next greatest place values. Stem and leaf plots are best suited for small sets of data and are especially useful for comparing two sets of data. The following is an example using test scores:

4	9
5	4 9
6	1 2 3 4 6 7 8 8
7	0 3 4 6 6 6 7 7 7 8 8 8 8
8	3 5 5 7 8
9	0 0 3 4 5
10	0 0

Histograms are used to summarize information from large sets of data that can be naturally grouped into intervals. The vertical axis indicates **frequency** (the number of times any particular data value occurs), and the horizontal axis indicates data values or ranges of data values. The number of data values in any interval is the **frequency of the interval**.

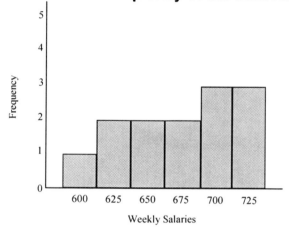

COMPETENCY 10.0 GRAPH NUMBERS OR NUMBER RELATIONSHIPS

Skill 10.1   Identify points from their coordinates, the coordinates of points, or graphs of sets of ordered pairs.

Coordinate plane - A plane with a point selected as an origin, some length selected as a unit of distance, and two perpendicular lines that intersect at the origin, with positive and negative direction selected on each line. Traditionally, the lines are called x (drawn from left to right, with positive direction to the right of the origin) and y (drawn from bottom to top, with positive direction upward of the origin). Coordinates of a point are determined by the distance of this point from the lines, and the signs of the coordinates are determined by whether the point is in the positive or in the negative direction from the origin. The standard coordinate plane consists of a plane divided into 4 quadrants by the intersection of two axis, the *x*-axis (horizontal axis), and the *y*-axis (vertical axis).

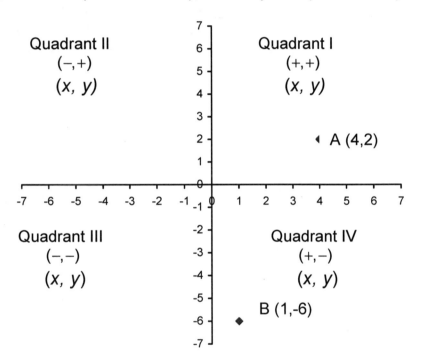

Coordinates - A unique **ordered pair** of numbers that identifies a point on the coordinate plane. The first number in the ordered pair identifies the position with regard to the x-axis while the second number identifies the position on the y-axis (*x* ,*y*)

In the coordinate plane shown above, point A has the ordered pair (4,2); point B has the ordered pair (1,-6).

Skill 10.2   Identify the graphs of equations or inequalities, and find the slopes and intercepts of lines.

Slope – The slope of a line is the "slant" of a line. A downward left to right slant means a negative slope. An upward slant is a positive slope.
The formula for calculating the slope of a line with coordinates $(x_1, y_1) and (x_2, y_2)$ is:

$$slope = \frac{y_2 - y_1}{x_2 - x_1}$$

The top of the fraction represents the change in the y coordinates; it is called the **rise**.
The bottom of the fraction represents the change in the x coordinates, it is called the **run.**

Example: Find the slope of a line with points at (2,2) and (7,8).

$\frac{(8)-(2)}{(7)-(2)}$ plug the values into the formula

$\frac{6}{5}$ solve the rise over run

$= 1.2$ solve for the slope

The length of a line segment is the **distance** between two different points, A and B. The formula for the length of a line is:

$$length = \sqrt{(x_1 - x_2)^2 + (y_1 - y_2)^2}$$

Example: Find the length between the points (2,2) and (7,8)

$= \sqrt{(2-7)^2 + (2-8)^2}$ plug the values into the formula

$= \sqrt{(-5)^2 + (-6)^2}$ calculate the x and y differences

$= \sqrt{25 + 36}$ square the values

$= \sqrt{61}$ add the two values

$= 7.81$ calculate the square root

A first degree equation has an equation of the form $ax + by = c$. To find the slope of a line, solve the equation for y. This gets the equation into **slope intercept form**, $y = mx + b$. **m is the line's slope.**

The y intercept is the coordinate of the point where a line crosses the y axis. To find the y intercept, substitute 0 for x and solve for y. This is the y intercept. In slope intercept form, $y = mx + b$, b is the y intercept.

To find the x intercept, substitute 0 for y and solve for x. This is the x intercept.

If the equation solves to $x =$ **any number**, then the graph is a **vertical line**. It only has an x intercept. Its slope is **undefined**.

If the equation solves to $y =$ **any number**, then the graph is a **horizontal line**. It only has a y intercept. Its slope is 0 (zero).

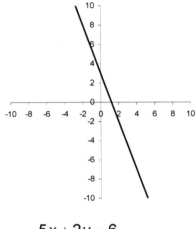

$$5x + 2y = 6$$
$$y = {}^{-}5/2\,x + 3$$

The equation of a line from its graph can be found by finding its slope (see Skill 3.2 for the slope formula) and its y intercept.

$$Y - y_a = m(X - x_a)$$

(x_a, y_a) can be (x_1, y_1) or (x_2, y_2) If **m**, the value of the slope, is distributed through the parentheses, the equation can be rewritten into other forms of the equation of a line.

Example: Find the equation of a line through $(9, {}^-6)$ and $({}^-1, 2)$.

$$\text{slope} = \frac{y_2 - y_1}{x_2 - x_1} = \frac{2 - {}^-6}{{}^-1 - 9} = \frac{8}{{}^-10} = \frac{{}^-4}{5}$$

$$Y - y_a = m(X - x_a) \rightarrow Y - 2 = {}^-4/5(X - {}^-1) \rightarrow$$

$$Y - 2 = {}^-4/5(X + 1) \rightarrow Y - 2 = {}^-4/5\,X - 4/5 \rightarrow$$

$$Y = {}^-4/5\ X + 6/5 \quad \text{This is the slope-intercept form.}$$

Multiplying by 5 to eliminate fractions, it is:

$$5Y = {}^-4X + 6 \rightarrow 4X + 5Y = 6 \quad \text{Standard form.}$$

Example: Find the slope and intercepts of $3x + 2y = 14$.

$$3x + 2y = 14$$
$$2y = {}^-3x + 14$$
$$y = {}^-3/2\ x + 7$$

The slope of the line is ${}^-3/2$. The y intercept of the line is 7.

The intercepts can also be found by substituting 0 in place of the other variable in the equation.

To find the y intercept:	To find the x intercept:
let $x = 0$; $3(0) + 2y = 14$	let $y = 0$; $3x + 2(0) = 14$
$0 + 2y = 14$	$3x + 0 = 14$
$2y = 14$	$3x = 14$
$y = 7$	$x = 14/3$
$(0,7)$ is the y intercept.	$(14/3, 0)$ is the x intercept.

Example: Sketch the graph of the line represented by $2x + 3y = 6$.

Let $x = 0 \rightarrow 2(0) + 3y = 6$
$\rightarrow 3y = 6$
$\rightarrow y = 2$
$\rightarrow (0,2)$ is the y intercept.

Let $y = 0 \rightarrow 2x + 3(0) = 6$
$\rightarrow 2x = 6$
$\rightarrow x = 3$
$\rightarrow (3,0)$ is the x intercept.

Let $x = 1 \rightarrow 2(1) + 3y = 6$
$\rightarrow 2 + 3y = 6$
$\rightarrow 3y = 4$
$\rightarrow y = \dfrac{4}{3}$
$\rightarrow \left(1, \dfrac{4}{3}\right)$ is the third point.

Plotting the three points on the coordinate system, we get the following:

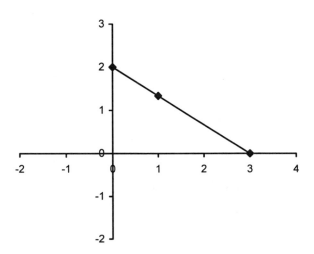

To graph an inequality, solve the inequality for y. This gets the inequality in **slope intercept form**, (for example: $y < mx + b$). The point (0,b) is the y-intercept and m is the line's slope.

If the inequality solves to $x \geq$ **any number**, then the graph includes a **vertical line**.

If the inequality solves to $y \leq$ **any number**, then the graph includes a **horizontal line**.

When graphing a linear inequality, the line will be dotted if the inequality sign is $<$ or $>$. If the inequality signs are either $\geq$ or $\leq$, the line on the graph will be a solid line. Shade above the line when the inequality sign is $\geq$ or $>$. Shade below the line when the inequality sign is $<$ or $\leq$. For inequalities of the forms $x >$ number, $x \leq$ number , $x <$ number ,or $x \geq$ number, draw a vertical line (solid or dotted). Shade to the right for $>$ or $\geq$. Shade to the left for $<$ or $\leq$.

Remember: **Dividing or multiplying by a negative number will reverse the direction of the inequality sign.**

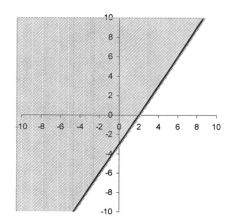

$$3x - 2y \geq 6$$
$$y \leq 3/2\,x - 3$$

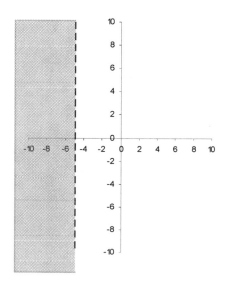

$$3x + 12 < -3$$
$$x < {}^-5$$

Example: Solve by graphing:

$$x + y \leq 6$$
$$x - 2y \leq 6$$

Solving the inequalities for y, they become:

$y \leq {}^-x + 6$ (y intercept of 6 and slope = $^-1$)

$y \geq 1/2\,x - 3$ (y intercept of $^-3$ and slope = $1/2$)

A graph with shading is shown below:

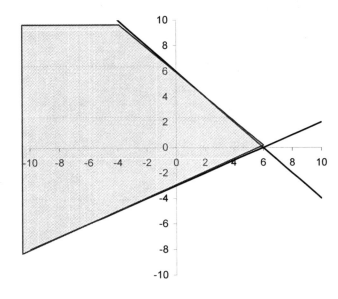

Skill 10.3   Recognize direct and inverse variation presented graphically.

If two things vary directly, as one gets larger, the other also gets larger. If one gets smaller, then the other gets smaller too. If x and y vary directly, there should be a constant, c, such that $y = cx$. Something can also vary directly with the square of something else, $y = cx^2$.

If two things vary inversely, as one gets larger, the other one gets smaller instead. If x and y vary inversely, there should be a constant, c, such that $xy = c$ or $y = c/x$. Something can also vary inversely with the square of something else, $y = c/x^2$.

Example: If $30 is paid for 5 hours work, how much would be paid for 19 hours work?

This is direct variation and $30 = 5c, so the constant is 6 ($6/hour). So $y = 6(19)$ or y = $114.

This could also be done as a proportion: $\dfrac{\$30}{5} = \dfrac{y}{19}$

$5y = 570$
$y = 114$

Example: On a 546 mile trip from Miami to Charlotte, one car drove 65 mph while another car drove 70 mph. How does this affect the driving time for the trip?

This is an inverse variation, since increasing your speed should decrease your driving time. Using the equation: rate × time = distance, rt = d.

65t = 546   and   70t = 546
t = 8.4   and   t = 7.8
slower speed, more time   faster speed, less time

Example: Consider the average monthly temperatures for a hypothetical location.

Month	Avg. Temp. (F)
Jan	40
March	48
May	65
July	81
Sept	80
Nov	60

Note that the graph of the average temperatures resembles the graph of a trigonometric function with a period of one year. We can use the periodic nature of seasonal temperature fluctuation to predict weather patterns.

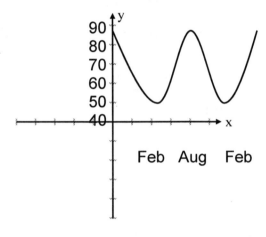

COMPETENCY 11.0 SOLVE ONE- AND TWO-VARIABLE EQUATIONS

Skill 11.1   Find the value of the unknown in one-variable equations.

Procedure for solving algebraic equations.

Example: $3(x+3) = {}^-2x + 4$ Solve for x.

1)   Expand to eliminate all parentheses.

$3x + 9 = {}^-2x + 4$

2)   Multiply each term by the LCD to eliminate all denominators.

3)   Combine like terms on each side when possible.

4)   Use the properties to put all variables on one side and all constants on the other side.

$\rightarrow 3x + 9 - 9 = {}^-2x + 4 - 9$ (subtract nine from both sides)

$\rightarrow 3x = {}^-2x - 5$

$\rightarrow 3x + 2x = {}^-2x + 2x - 5$ (add $2x$ to both sides)

$\rightarrow 5x = {}^-5$

$\rightarrow \dfrac{5x}{5} = \dfrac{{}^-5}{5}$ (divide both sides by 5)

$\rightarrow x = {}^-1$

Example: Solve: $3(2x + 5) - 4x = 5(x + 9)$

$6x + 15 - 4x = 5x + 45$

$2x + 15 = 5x + 45$

${}^-3x + 15 = 45$

${}^-3x = 30$

$x = {}^-10$

Skill 11.2   Solve a system of two linear equations in two variables.

The solution **set of linear equations** is all the ordered pairs of real numbers that satisfy both equations, thus the intersection of the lines There are two methods for solving linear equations: **linear combinations** and **substitution**.

In the **substitution** method, an equation is solved for either variable. Then, that solution is substituted in the other equation to find the remaining variable.

Example:

(1) $2x + 8y = 4$
(2) $x - 3y = 5$

(2a) $x = 3y + 5$ Solve equation (2) for x

(1a) $2(3y + 5) + 8y = 4$ Substitute x in equation (1)
        $6y + 10 + 8y = 4$ Solve.
        $14y = -6$
        $y = \frac{-3}{7}$ Solution

(2) $x - 3y = 5$
       $x - 3(\frac{-3}{7}) = 5$ Substitute the value of y.
       $x = \frac{26}{7} = 3\frac{5}{7}$ Solution

Thus the solution set of the system of equations is $(3\frac{5}{7}, \frac{-3}{7})$.

In the **linear combinations** method, one or both of the equations are replaced with an equivalent equation in order that the two equations can be combined (added or subtracted) to eliminate one variable.

Example:

(1) $4x + 3y = -2$
(2) $5x - y = 7$
(1) $4x + 3y = -2$
(2a) $15x - 3y = 21$ Multiply equation (2) by 3
       $19x = 19$ Combining (1) and (2a)
       $x = 1$ Solve.
To find y, substitute the value of x in equation 1 (or 2).
(1) $4x + 3y = -2$
       $4(1) + 3y = -2$
       $4 + 3y = -2$
       $3y = -2$
       $y = -2$
Thus the solution is $x = 1$ and $y = -2$ or the order pair (1, -2).

Example: Solve for x and y.

$$4x + 6y = 340$$
$$3x + 8y = 360$$

To solve by addition-subtraction:

Multiply the first equation by 4: $4(4x + 6y = 340)$

Multiply the other equation by $^-3$: $^-3(3x + 8y = 360)$

By doing this, the equations can be added to each other to eliminate one variable and solve for the other variable.

$$16x + 24y = 1360$$
$$\underline{-9x - 24y = {}^-1080}$$
$$7x = 280$$
$$x = 40$$

solving for y, $y = 30$

COMPETENCY 12.0 SOLVE WORD PROBLEMS INVOLVING ONE AND TWO VARIABLES

Skill 12.1 **Solve word problems that can be translated into one-variable linear equations or systems of two-variable linear equations.**

Example: Mark and Mike are twins. Three times Mark's age plus four equals four times Mike's age minus 14. How old are the boys?

Since the boys are twins, their ages are the same. "Translate" the English into Algebra. Let x = their age

$3x + 4 = 4x - 14$

$18 = x$

The boys are each 18 years old.

Example: The YMCA wants to sell raffle tickets to raise $32,000. If they must pay $7,250 in expenses and prizes out of the money collected from the tickets, how many tickets worth $25 each must they sell?

Let x = number of tickets sold
Then $25x$ = total money collected for x tickets

Total money minus expenses is greater than $32,000.

$25x - 7250 = 32,000$
$25x = 39350$
$x = 1570$

If they sell 1,570 tickets, they will raise $32,000.

Example: The Simpsons went out for dinner. All 4 of them ordered the aardvark steak dinner. Bert paid for the 4 meals and included a tip of $12 for a total of $84.60. How much was an aardvark steak dinner?

Let x = the price of one aardvark dinner.
So $4x$ = the price of 4 aardvark dinners.

$$4x + 12 = 84.60$$
$$4x = 72.60$$
$$x = \$18.15 \text{ for each dinner.}$$

Some word problems can be solved using a system (group) of equations or inequalities. Watch for words like greater than, less than, at least, or no more than which indicate the need for inequalities.

Example: Farmer Greenjeans bought 4 cows and 6 sheep for $1700. Mr. Ziffel bought 3 cows and 12 sheep for $2400. If all the cows were the same price and all the sheep were another price, find the price charged for a cow or for a sheep.

Let x = price of a cow
Let y = price of a sheep

Then Farmer Greenjeans' equation would be: $4x + 6y = 1700$
Mr. Ziffel's equation would be: $3x + 12y = 2400$

To solve by **addition-subtraction**:
Multiply the first equation by $^-2$: $^-2(4x + 6y = 1700)$
Keep the other equation the same : $(3x + 12y = 2400)$
By doing this, the equations can be added to each other to eliminate one variable and solve for the other variable.

$$^-8x - 12y = {}^-3400$$
$$\underline{3x + 12y = 2400} \qquad \text{Add these equations.}$$
$$^-5x \qquad = {}^-1000$$

$x = 200 \leftarrow$ the price of a cow was $200.
Solving for y, $y = 150 \leftarrow$ the price of a sheep, $150.

To solve by **substitution**:

Solve one of the equations for a variable. (Try to make an equation without fractions if possible.) Substitute this expression into the equation that you have not yet used. Solve the resulting equation for the value of the remaining variable.

$$4x + 6y = 1700$$
$$3x + 12y = 2400 \leftarrow \text{Solve this equation for } x.$$

It becomes $x = 800 - 4y$. Now substitute $800 - 4y$ in place of x in the OTHER equation. $4x + 6y = 1700$ now becomes:

$$4(800 - 4y) + 6y = 1700$$
$$3200 - 16y + 6y = 1700$$
$$3200 - 10y = 1700$$
$$^-10y = {}^-1500$$
$$y = 150, \text{ or } \$150 \text{ for a sheep.}$$

Substituting 150 back into an equation for y, find x.
$$4x + 6(150) = 1700$$
$$4x + 900 = 1700$$
$$4x = 800 \text{ so } x = 200 \text{ for a cow.}$$

Example: Sharon's Bike Shoppe can assemble a 3 speed bike in 30 minutes or a 10 speed bike in 60 minutes. The profit on each bike sold is $60 for a 3 speed or $75 for a 10 speed bike. How many of each type of bike should they assemble during an 8 hour day (480 minutes) to make the maximum profit? Total daily profit must be at least $300.

Let $x =$ number of 3 speed bikes.
  $y =$ number of 10 speed bikes.

Since there are only 480 minutes to use each day,

  $30x + 60y \leq 480$ is the first inequality.

Since the total daily profit must be at least $300,

  $60x + 75y \geq 300$ is the second inequality.

  $32x + 65y \leq 480$ solves to $y \leq 8 - 1/2x$
  $60x + 75y \geq 300$ solves to $y \geq 4 - 4/5x$

Graph these 2 inequalities:

$$y \leq 8 - 1/2\,x$$
$$y \geq 4 - 4/5\,x$$

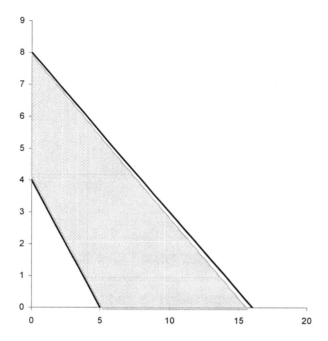

Realize that $x \geq 0$ and $y \geq 0$, since the number of bikes assembled can not be a negative number. Graph these as additional constraints on the problem. The number of bikes assembled must always be an integer value, so points within the shaded area of the graph must have integer values. The maximum profit will occur at or near a corner of the shaded portion of this graph. Those points occur at (0,4), (0,8), (16,0), or (5,0).

Since profits are $60/3$-speed or $75/10$-speed, the profit would be :

$$(0,4) \quad 60(0) + 75(4) = 300$$
$$(0,8) \quad 60(0) + 75(8) = 600$$
$$(16,0) \quad 60(16) + 75(0) = 960 \leftarrow \text{Maximum profit}$$
$$(5,0) \quad 60(5) + 75(0) = 300$$

The maximum profit would occur if 16 3-speed bikes are made daily.

COMPETENCY 13.0 UNDERSTAND OPERATIONS WITH ALGEBRAIC EXPRESSIONS

Skill 13.1   Factor quadratics and polynomials.

A **quadratic equation** is written in the form $ax^2 + bx + c = 0$. To solve a quadratic equation by factoring, at least one of the factors must equal zero.

Example: $3x^2 - 20x - 7$ has two factors.

$(3x + 1)$ and $(x - 7)$

To confirm, we use the FOIL method.

$(3x + 1)(x - 7)$
   a   b c   d

1. F= multiply the First terms (a and c) $\rightarrow 3x \cdot x = 3x^2$

2. O=multiply the Outside terms (a and d) $\rightarrow 3x \cdot {}^- 7 = {}^- 21x$

3. I=multiply the Inside terms (b and c) $\rightarrow 1 \cdot x = x$
    Add the inside and outside answers $\rightarrow {}^- 21x + x = {}^- 20x$

4. L=multiply the Last terms $\rightarrow 1 \cdot {}^- 7 = {}^- 7$

Corresponding to $3x^2 - 20x - 7$

Example: Solve the equation.

$x^2 + 10x - 24 = 0$
$(x + 12)(x - 2) = 0$ Factor.
$x + 12 = 0$ or $x - 2 = 0$ Set each factor equal to 0.
$x = {}^- 12$ $x = 2$ Solve.

Check:
$x^2 + 10x - 24 = 0$
$({}^- 12)^2 + 10({}^- 12) - 24 = 0$ $(2)^2 + 10(2) - 24 = 0$
$144 - 120 - 24 = 0$ $4 + 20 - 24 = 0$
$0 = 0$ $0 = 0$

A quadratic equation that cannot be solved by factoring can be solved by completing the square.

Example: Solve the equation.

$$x^2 - 6x + 8 = 0$$

$$x^2 - 6x = \,^-8$$ Move the constant to the right side.

$$x^2 - 6x + 9 = \,^-8 + 9$$ Add the square of half the cooeffient of x to both sides.

$$(x - 3)^2 = 1$$ Write the left side as a perfect square.

$$x - 3 = \pm\sqrt{1}$$ Take the square root of both sides.

$x - 3 = 1$	$x - 3 = \,^-1$ Solve.
$x = 4$	$x = 2$

Check:

$$x^2 - 6x + 8 = 0$$

$4^2 - 6(4) + 8 = 0$	$2^2 - 6(2) + 8 = 0$
$16 - 24 + 8 = 0$	$4 - 12 + 8 = 0$
$0 = 0$	$0 = 0$

The general technique for graphing quadratics is the same as for graphing linear equations. Graphing quadratic equations, however, results in a parabola instead of a straight line.

Example: Graph $y = 3x^2 + x - 2$.

x	$y = 3x^2 + x - 2$
$^-2$	8
$^-1$	0
0	$^-2$
1	2
2	12

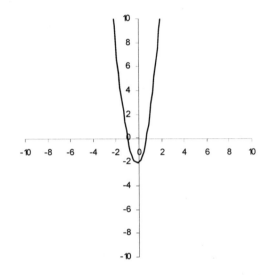

To solve a quadratic equation using the quadratic formula, be sure that your equation is in the form $ax^2 + bx + c = 0$. Substitute these values into the formula:

$$x = \frac{-b \pm \sqrt{b^2 - 4ac}}{2a}$$

Example: Solve the equation.

$$3x^2 = 7 + 2x \rightarrow 3x^2 - 2x - 7 = 0$$

$$a = 3 \quad b = {}^-2 \quad c = {}^-7$$

$$x = \frac{-({}^-2) \pm \sqrt{({}^-2)^2 - 4(3)({}^-7)}}{2(3)}$$

$$x = \frac{2 \pm \sqrt{4 + 84}}{6}$$

$$x = \frac{2 \pm \sqrt{88}}{6}$$

$$x = \frac{2 \pm 2\sqrt{22}}{6}$$

$$x = \frac{1 \pm \sqrt{22}}{3}$$

Factoring polynomials

GCF is the abbreviation for the **greatest common factor**. The GCF is the largest number that is a factor of all the numbers given in a problem. The GCF can be no larger than the smallest number given in the problem. If no other number is a common factor, then the GCF will be the number 1. To find the GCF, list all possible factors of the smallest number given (include the number itself). Starting with the largest factor (which is the number itself), determine if it is also a factor of all the other given numbers. If so, that is the GCF. If that factor doesn't work, try the same method on the next smaller factor. Continue until a common factor is found. That is the GCF. Note: There can be other common factors besides the GCF.

Example: Find the GCF of 12, 20, and 36.

The smallest number in the problem is 12. The factors of 12 are 1,2,3,4,6 and 12. 12 is the largest factor, but it does not divide evenly into 20. Neither does 6, but 4 will divide into both 20 and 36 evenly.

Therefore, 4 is the GCF.

Example: Find the GCF of 14 and 15.

Factors of 14 are 1,2,7 and 14. 14 is the largest factor, but it does not divide evenly into 15. Neither does 7 or 2. Therefore, the only factor common to both 14 and 15 is the number 1, the GCF.

LCM is the abbreviation for **least common multiple**. The least common multiple of a group of numbers is the smallest number that all of the given numbers will divide into. The least common multiple will always be the largest of the given numbers or a multiple of the largest number.

Example: Find the LCM of 20, 30 and 40.

The largest number given is 40, but 30 will not divide evenly into 40. The next multiple of 40 is 80 (2 x 40), but 30 will not divide evenly into 80 either. The next multiple of 40 is 120. 120 is divisible by both 20 and 30, so 120 is the LCM (least common multiple).

Example: Find the LCM of 96, 16 and 24.

The largest number is 96. 96 is divisible by both 16 and 24, so 96 is the LCM.

Example: Elly Mae can feed the animals in 15 minutes. Jethro can feed them in 10 minutes. How long will it take them if they work together?

If Elly Mae can feed the animals in 15 minutes, then she could feed 1/15 of them in 1 minute, 2/15 of them in 2 minutes, $x/15$ of them in x minutes. In the same fashion Jethro could feed $x/10$ of them in x minutes. Together they complete 1 job. The equation is:

$$\frac{x}{15} + \frac{x}{10} = 1$$

Multiply each term by the LCD of 30:

$$2x + 3x = 30$$
$$x = 6 \text{ minutes}$$

To factor the sum or the difference of perfect cubes, follow this procedure:
a. Factor out any greatest common factor (GCF).
b. Make a parentheses for a binomial (2 terms) followed by a trinomial (3 terms).
c. The sign in the first parentheses is the same as the sign in the problem. The difference of cubes will have a "-" sign in the first parentheses. The sum of cubes will use a "+".
  d. The first sign in the second parentheses is the opposite of the sign in the first parentheses. The second sign in the other parentheses is always a "+".
e. Determine what would be cubed to equal each term of the problem. Put those expressions in the first parentheses.

f. To make the 3 terms of the trinomial, think square - product - square. Looking at the binomial, square the first term. This is the trinomial's first term. Looking at the binomial, find the product of the two terms, ignoring the signs. This is the trinomial's second term. Looking at the binomial, square the third term. This is the trinomial's third term. Except in rare instances, the trinomial does not factor again.

Example: Factor completely:

1.

$16x^3 + 54y^3$

$2(8x^3 + 27y^3)$ $\leftarrow$ GCF

$2(\quad + \quad)(\quad - \quad + \quad)$ $\leftarrow$ signs

$2(2x+3y)(\quad - \quad + \quad)$ $\leftarrow$ what is cubed to equal $8x^3$ or $27y^3$

$2(2x+3y)(4x^2 - 6xy + 9y^2)$ $\leftarrow$ square-product-square

2.

$64a^3 - 125b^3$

$(\quad - \quad)(\quad + \quad + \quad)$ $\leftarrow$ signs

$(4a-5b)(\quad + \quad + \quad)$ $\leftarrow$ what is cubed to equal $64a^3$ or $125b^3$

$(4a-5b)(16a^2 + 20ab + 25b^2)$ $\leftarrow$ square-product-square

3.
$$27x^{27} + 343y^{12} = (3x^9 + 7y^{12})(9x^{18} - 21x^9y^{12} + 49y^{24})$$
Note: The coefficient 27 is different from the exponent 27.

Skill 13.2   Add, subtract, and multiply polynomial expressions.

Polynomial expressions are of the form ax^k, where k is the degree of the polynomial and a is the coefficient. Whether you are adding, subtracting, or multiplying polynomials, it is always best to write them in standard form; i.e. with the highest degree polynomial first and the others in descending order.

To add two polynomials, add the coefficients of like terms.

Example: Add $4x^2 + 2x - 10$ and $2x^2 + 2x + 12$

$$\left(4x^2 + 2x - 10\right) + \left(2x^2 + 2x + 12\right) =$$

Solution: $$\left(4x^2 + 2x^2\right) + \left(2x + 2x\right) + \left(-10 + 12\right) =$$

$$6x^2 + 4x + 2$$

To subtract a polynomial, you must subtract each of its terms.

Example: Subtract $4x^2 - 2x - 8$ from $6x^2 - 10x + 6$

$$\left(6x^2 - 10x + 6\right) - \left(4x^2 - 2x - 8\right) =$$

Solution: $$6x^2 - 10x + 6 - 4x^2 + 2x + 8 =$$

$$\left(6x^2 - 4x^2\right) + \left(-10x + 2x\right) + \left(6 + 8\right) =$$

$$2x^2 - 8x + 14$$

To multiply two polynomials, each term of one polynomial must be multiplied by each term of the other polynomial.

Example: Multiply: $\left(2x^2 - 3x - 2\right)(x - 10)$

$$\left(2x^2 - 3x - 2\right)(x - 10) =$$

Solution: $$2x^2(x - 10) - 3x(x - 10) - 2(x - 10) =$$

$$2x^3 - 20x^2 - 3x^2 + 30x - 2x + 10 =$$

$$2x^3 - 23x^2 + 28x + 10$$

Skill 13.3   **Perform basic operations on and simplifying rational expressions.**

Add or subtract rational algebraic fractions.

In order to add or subtract rational expressions, they must have a common denominator. If they don't have a common denominator, then factor the denominators to determine what factors are missing from each denominator to make the LCD. Multiply both numerator and denominator by the missing factor(s). Once the fractions have a common denominator, add or subtract their numerators, but keep the common denominator the same. Factor the numerator if possible and reduce if there are any factors that can be cancelled.

Example: Find the least common denominator for $6a^3b^2$ and $4ab^3$.

These factor into $2 \cdot 3 \cdot a^3 \cdot b^2$ and $2 \cdot 2 \cdot a \cdot b^3$.
The first expression must be multiplied by another 2 and b.
 The other expression must be multiplied by 3 and a^2.
 Then both expressions would be
$2 \cdot 2 \cdot 3 \cdot a^3 \cdot b^3 = 12a^3b^3 = \text{LCD}$.

Example: Find the LCD for $x^2 - 4$, $x^2 + 5x + 6$, and $x^2 + x - 6$.

$x^2 - 4$ factors into $(x - 2)(x + 2)$

$x^2 + 5x + 6$ factors into $(x + 3)(x + 2)$

$x^2 + x - 6$ factors into $(x + 3)(x - 2)$

To make these lists of factors the same, they must all be $(x + 3)(x + 2)(x - 2)$. This is the LCD.

Example: Solve

$$\frac{5}{6a^3b^2} + \frac{1}{4ab^3} = \frac{5(2b)}{6a^3b^2(2b)} + \frac{1(3a^2)}{4ab^3(3a^2)} = \frac{10a}{12a^3b^3} + \frac{3b^2}{12a^3b^3} = \frac{10a + 3b^2}{12a^3b^3}$$

This will not reduce as all 3 terms are not divisible by anything.

Example:　Solve

$$\frac{2}{x^2-4} - \frac{3}{x^2+5x+6} + \frac{7}{x^2+x-6} =$$

$$\frac{2}{(x-2)(x+2)} - \frac{3}{(x+3)(x+2)} + \frac{7}{(x+3)(x-2)} =$$

$$\frac{2(x+3)}{(x-2)(x+2)(x+3)} - \frac{3(x-2)}{(x+3)(x+2)(x-2)} + \frac{7(x+2)}{(x+3)(x-2)(x+2)} =$$

$$\frac{2x+6}{(x-2)(x+2)(x+3)} - \frac{3x-6}{(x+3)(x+2)(x-2)} + \frac{7x+14}{(x+3)(x-2)(x+2)} =$$

$$\frac{2x+6-(3x-6)+7x+14}{(x+3)(x-2)(x+2)} = \frac{6x+26}{(x+3)(x-2)(x+2)}$$

This will not reduce.

COMPETENCY 14.0 SOLVE PROBLEMS INVOLVING GEOMETRIC FIGURES

Skill 14.1 **Identify the appropriate formula for solving geometric problems; solve problems involving two- and three-dimensional geometric figures.**

Polygons, simple closed **two-dimensional figures** composed of line segments, are named according to the number of sides they have.

A **quadrilateral** is a polygon with four sides.
The sum of the measures of the angles of a quadrilateral is 360°.

A **trapezoid** is a quadrilateral with exactly <u>one</u> pair of parallel sides.

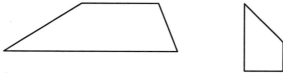

In an **isosceles trapezoid**, the non-parallel sides are congruent.

A **parallelogram** is a quadrilateral with <u>two</u> pairs of parallel sides.

In a parallelogram:
The diagonals bisect each other.
Each diagonal divides the parallelogram into two congruent triangles.
Both pairs of opposite sides are congruent.
Both pairs of opposite angles are congruent.
Two adjacent angles are supplementary.

A **rectangle** is a parallelogram with a right angle.

A **rhombus** is a parallelogram with all sides equal length.

A **square** is a rectangle with all sides equal length.

Example: True or false?

All squares are rhombuses.	True
All parallelograms are rectangles.	False - <u>some</u> parallelograms are rectangles
All rectangles are parallelograms.	True
Some rhombuses are squares.	True
Some rectangles are trapezoids.	False - only <u>one</u> pair of parallel sides
All quadrilaterals are parallelograms.	False -some quadrilaterals are parallelograms
Some squares are rectangles.	False - all squares are rectangles
Some parallelograms are rhombuses.	True

A **triangle** is a polygon with three sides.

Triangles can be classified by the types of angles or the lengths of their sides.

An **acute** triangle has exactly three *acute* angles.
A **right** triangle has one *right* angle.
An **obtuse** triangle has one *obtuse* angle.

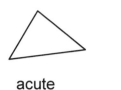   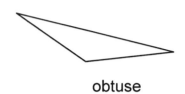

       acute   right   obtuse

All *three* sides of an **equilateral** triangle are the same length.
Two sides of an **isosceles** triangle are the same length.
None of the sides of a **scalene** triangle are the same length.

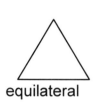   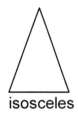   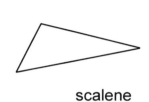

    equilateral   isosceles   scalene

Example: Can a triangle have two right angles?
              No. A right angle measures $90°$, therefore the sum of two right angles would be $180°$ and there could not be third angle.

Example: Can a triangle have two obtuse angles?
              No. Since an obtuse angle measures more than $90°$ the sum of two obtuse angles would be greater than $180°$.

A **cylinder** has two congruent circular bases that are parallel.

A **sphere** is a space figure having all its points the same distance from the center.

A **cone** is a space figure having a circular base and a single vertex.

A **pyramid** is a space figure with a square base and 4 triangle-shaped sides.

A **tetrahedron** is a 4-sided space triangle. Each face is a triangle.

A **prism** is a space figure with two congruent, parallel bases that are polygons.

FIGURE	AREA FORMULA	PERIMETER FORMULA
Rectangle	LW	$2(L+W)$
Triangle	$\dfrac{1}{2}bh$	$a+b+c$
Parallelogram	bh	sum of lengths of sides
Trapezoid	$\dfrac{1}{2}h(a+b)$	sum of lengths of sides

Perimeter

Example: A farmer has a piece of land shaped as shown below. He wishes to fence this land at an estimated cost of $25 per linear foot. What is the total cost of fencing this property to the nearest foot.

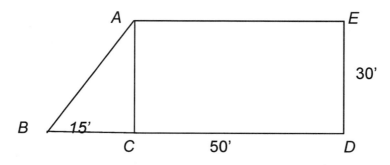

From the right triangle ABC, AC = 30 and BC = 15.

Since $(AB) = (AC)^2 + (BC)^2$
$(AB) = (30)^2 + (15)^2$

So $\sqrt{(AB)^2} = AB = \sqrt{1125} = 33.5410$ feet

To the nearest foot AB = 34 feet.

Perimeter of the piece of land is $= AB + BC + CD + DE + EA$

$= 34 + 15 + 50 + 30 + 50 = 179$ feet

cost of fencing = $25 x 179 = $4, 475.00

Area

Area is the space that a figure occupies. Example:

Example: What will be the cost of carpeting a rectangular office that measures 12 feet by 15 feet if the carpet costs $12.50 per square yard?

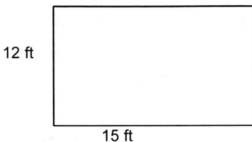

12 ft

15 ft

The problem is asking you to determine the area of the office. The area of a rectangle is *length x width = A*

Substitute the given values in the equation *A = lw*
A = (12 ft.)(15 ft.)
A = 180 ft.

The problem asked you to determine the cost of carpet at $12.50 per square yard.

First, you need to convert 180 ft.^{2} into yards^2.

1 yd. = 3 ft.
$$(1 \text{ yard})(1 \text{ yard}) = (3 \text{ feet})(3 \text{ feet})$$
$$1 \text{ yd}^2 = 9 \text{ ft } 2$$

Hence, $\dfrac{180 \text{ ft}^2}{1} = \dfrac{1 \text{ yd}^2}{9 \text{ ft}^2} = \dfrac{20}{1} = 20 \text{ yd}^2$

The carpet cost $12.50 per square yard; thus the cost of carpeting the office described is $12.50 x 20 = $250.00.

Example: Find the area of a parallelogram whose base is 6.5 cm and the height of the altitude to that base is 3.7 cm.

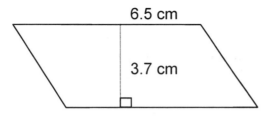

6.5 cm

3.7 cm

$A_{parallelogram}$ = bh

$$= (3.7)(6.5)$$
$$= 24.05 \text{ cm}^2$$

Example: Find the area of this triangle.

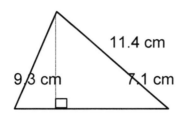

11.4 cm

9.3 cm   7.1 cm

16.8 cm

$A_{triangle} = \frac{1}{2}bh$

$$= 0.5\,(16.8)\,(7.1)$$
$$= 59.64 \text{ cm}^2$$

Example: Find the area of this trapezoid.

17.5 cm

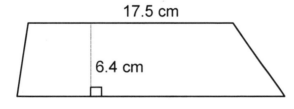

6.4 cm

23.7 cm

The area of a trapezoid equals one-half the sum of the bases times the altitude.

$A_{trapezoid} = \frac{1}{2}h(b_1 + b_2)$

$$= 0.5\,(6.4)\,(17.5 + 23.7)$$
$$= 131.84 \text{ cm}^2$$

The distance around a circle is the **circumference**. The ratio of the circumference to the diameter is represented by the Greek letter pi. $\Pi \sim 3.14$ $\sim \frac{22}{7}$.

The circumference of a circle is found by the formula $C = 2\Pi r$ or $C = \Pi d$ where r is the radius of the circle and d is the diameter.

The **area** of a circle is found by the formula $A = \Pi r^2$.

Example: Find the circumference and area of a circle whose radius is 7 meters.

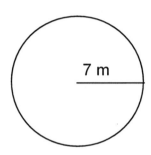

7 m

$C = 2\Pi r$
$= 2(3.14)(7)$
$= 43.96$ m

$A = \Pi r^2$
$= 3.14(7)(7)$
$= 153.86$ m^2

Volume and **Surface area** are computed using the following formulas:

FIGURE	VOLUME	TOTAL SURFACE AREA
Right Cylinder	$\pi r^2 h$	$2\pi rh + 2\pi r^2$
Right Cone	$\dfrac{\pi r^2 h}{3}$	$\pi r\sqrt{r^2 + h^2} + \pi r^2$
Sphere	$\dfrac{4}{3}\pi r^3$	$4\pi r^2$
Rectangular Solid	LWH	$2LW + 2WH + 2LH$

FIGURE	LATERAL AREA	TOTAL AREA	VOLUME
Regular Pyramid	1/2Pl	1/2Pl+B	1/3Bh

P = Perimeter
h = height
B = Area of Base
l = slant height

Example: What is the volume of a shoe box with a length of 35 cms, a width of 20 cms and a height of 15 cms?

Volume of a rectangular solid
= Length x Width x Height
= 35 x 20 x 15
= 10500 cm^3

Example: A water company is trying to decide whether to use traditional cylindrical paper cups or to offer conical paper cups since both cost the same. The traditional cups are 8 cm wide and 14 cm high. The conical cups are 12 cm wide and 19 cm high. The company will use the cup that holds the most water.

Draw and label a sketch of each.

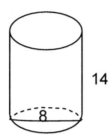 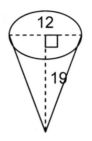

$$V = \pi r^2 h \qquad\qquad V = \frac{\pi r^2 h}{3} \qquad\qquad \text{1. write formula}$$

$$V = \pi(4)^2(14) \qquad\qquad V = \frac{1}{3}\pi(6)^2(19) \qquad\qquad \text{2. substitute}$$

$$V = 703.717 \text{ cm}^3 \qquad\qquad V = 716.283 \text{ cm}^3 \qquad\qquad \text{3. solve}$$

The choice should be the conical cup since its volume is more.

Example: How much material is needed to make a basketball that has a diameter of 15 inches? How much air is needed to fill the basketball?

Draw and label a sketch:

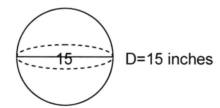 D=15 inches

Total surface area   Volume

$$\text{TSA} = 4\pi r^2 \qquad\qquad V = \frac{4}{3}\pi r^3 \qquad\qquad \text{1. write formula}$$

$$= 4\pi(7.5)^2 \qquad\qquad = \frac{4}{3}\pi(7.5)^3 \qquad\qquad \text{2. substitute}$$

$$= 706.858 \text{ in}^2 \qquad\qquad = 1767.1459 \text{ in}^3 \qquad\qquad \text{3. solve}$$

Skill 14.2 **Solve problems involving right triangles using the Pythagorean theorem.**

The Pythagorean Theorem states that given any right-angles triangle, $\triangle ABC$, the square of the hypotenuse is equal to the sum of the squares of the other two sides.

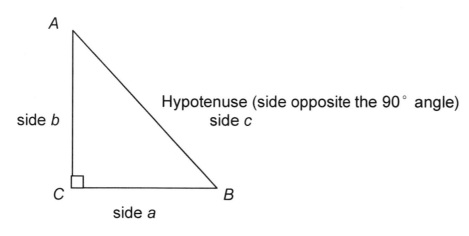

This theorem says that $(AB)^2 = (BC)^2 + (AC)^2$

or

$c^2 = a^2 + b^2$

Example: Find the area and perimeter of a rectangle if its length is 12 inches and its diagonal is 15 inches.

1. Draw and label sketch.

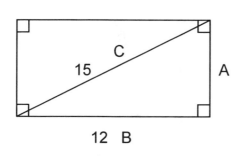

2. Since the height is still needed use Pythagorean formula to find missing leg of the triangle.

$A^2 + B^2 = C^2$
$A^2 + 12^2 = 15^2$
$A^2 = 15^2 - 12^2$
$A^2 = 81$
$A = 9$

Now use this information to find the area and perimeter.

$A = LW$ $P = 2(L + W)$ 1. write formula
$A = (12)(9)$ $P = 2(12 + 9)$ 2. substitute
$A = 108 \text{ in}^2$ $P = 42$ inches   3. solve

Example: Two old cars leave a road intersection at the same time. One car traveled due north at 55 mph while the other car traveled due east. After 3 hours, the cars were 180 miles apart. Find the speed of the second car.

Using a right triangle to represent the problem we get the figure:

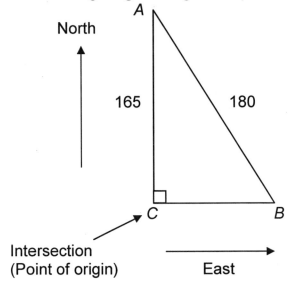

Traveling at 55 mph for 3 hours, the northbound car has driven (55)(3)=165 miles. This is the side *AC*.

We are given that the cars are 180 miles apart. This is side *AB*.

Since △*ABC* is a right triangle, then, by Pythagorean Theorem, we get:

$$(AB)^2 = (BC)^2 + (AC)^2 \text{ or}$$
$$(BC)^2 = (AB)^2 - (AC)^2$$

$$(BC)^2 = 180^2 - 165^2$$
$$(BC)^2 = 32400 - 27225$$
$$(BC)^2 = 5175$$

Take the square root of both sides to get:

$$\sqrt{(BC)^2} = \sqrt{5175} \approx 71.935 \text{ miles}$$

Since the east bound car has traveled 71.935 miles in 3 hours, then the average speed is:

$$\frac{71.935}{3} \approx 23.97 \text{ mph}$$

COMPETENCY 15.0 APPLY REASONING SKILLS

Skill 15.1   Draw conclusions using the principles of similarity, congruence, parallelism, and perpendicularity.

Congruent figures have the same size and shape. If one is placed above the other, it will fit exactly. Congruent lines have the same length. Congruent angles have equal measures. The symbol for congruent is $\cong$.

Polygons (pentagons) *ABCDE* and *VWXYZ* are congruent. They are exactly the same size and shape.

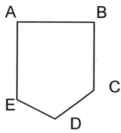

$$ABCDE \cong VWXYZ$$

Corresponding parts are those congruent angles and congruent sides, that is:

corresponding angles	corresponding sides
$\angle A \leftrightarrow \angle V$	$AB \leftrightarrow VW$
$\angle B \leftrightarrow \angle W$	$BC \leftrightarrow WX$
$\angle C \leftrightarrow \angle X$	$CD \leftrightarrow XY$
$\angle D \leftrightarrow \angle Y$	$DE \leftrightarrow YZ$
$\angle E \leftrightarrow \angle Z$	$AE \leftrightarrow VZ$

Example: Given two similar quadrilaterals. Find the lengths of sides *x, y,* and *z.*

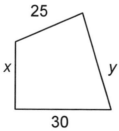
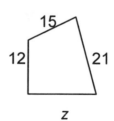

Since corresponding sides are proportional:

$$\frac{12}{x} = \frac{3}{5} \qquad \frac{21}{y} = \frac{3}{5} \qquad \frac{z}{30} = \frac{3}{5}$$

$$3x = 60 \qquad\quad 3y = 105 \qquad\quad 5z = 90$$
$$x = 20 \qquad\qquad y = 35 \qquad\qquad z = 18$$

Similarity

Two figures that have the same shape are **similar**. Polygons are similar if and only if corresponding angles are congruent and corresponding sides are in proportion. Corresponding parts of similar polygons are proportional.

Example: Given the rectangles below, compare the area and perimeter.

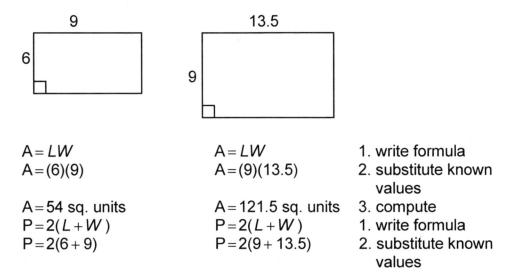

$A = LW$	$A = LW$	1. write formula
$A = (6)(9)$	$A = (9)(13.5)$	2. substitute known values
$A = 54$ sq. units	$A = 121.5$ sq. units	3. compute
$P = 2(L + W)$	$P = 2(L + W)$	1. write formula
$P = 2(6 + 9)$	$P = 2(9 + 13.5)$	2. substitute known values
$P = 30$ units	$P = 45$ units	3. compute

Notice that the areas relate to each other in the following manner:

Ratio of sides $9/13.5 = 2/3$

Multiply the first area by the square of the reciprocal $(3/2)^2$ to get the second area.

$$54 \times (3/2)^2 = 121.5$$

The perimeters relate to each other in the following manner:

Ratio of sides $9/13.5 = 2/3$

Multiply the perimeter of the first by the reciprocal of the ratio to get the perimeter of the second.

$$30 \times 3/2 = 45$$

Example: Tommy draws and cuts out 2 triangles for a school project. One of them has sides of 3, 6, and 9 inches. The other triangle has sides of 2, 4, and 6. Is there a relationship between the two triangles?

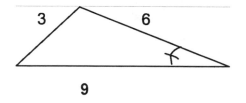

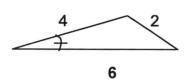

Take the proportion of the corresponding sides.

$$\frac{2}{3} \qquad \frac{4}{6} = \frac{2}{3} \qquad \frac{6}{9} = \frac{2}{3}$$

The smaller triangle is 2/3 the size of the large triangle.

Intersecting lines share a common point and intersecting planes share a common set of points or line.

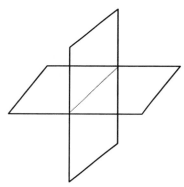

Skew lines do not intersect and do not lie on the same plane.

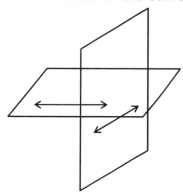

Perpendicular lines or planes form a 90 degree angle to each other.
Perpendicular lines have slopes that are negative reciprocals.

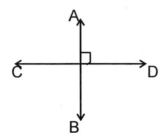

Line AB is perpendicular to line CD.

$AB \perp CD$

Parallel lines or planes do not intersect. Two parallel lines will have the same slope and are everywhere equidistant.

Line AB is parallel to line CD.

$AB \parallel CD$

Example: One line passes through the points (-4, -6) and (4, 6); another line passes through the points (-5, -4) and (3, 8). Are these lines parallel, perpendicular or neither?
Find the slopes.

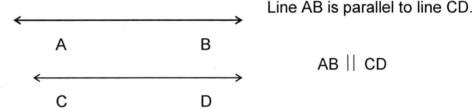

$$m = \frac{y_2 - y_1}{x_2 - x_1}$$

$$m_1 = \frac{6-(-6)}{4-(-4)} = \frac{6+6}{4+4} = \frac{12}{8} = \frac{3}{2}$$

$$m_2 = \frac{8-(-4)}{3-(-5)} = \frac{8+4}{3+5} = \frac{12}{8} = \frac{3}{2}$$

Since the slopes are the same, the lines are parallel.

Example: One line passes through the points (1, -3) and (0, -6); another line passes through the points (4, 1) and (-2, 3). Are these lines parallel, perpendicular or neither?
Find the slopes.

$$m = \frac{y_2 - y_1}{x_2 - x_1}$$

$$m_1 = \frac{-6-(-3)}{0-1} = \frac{-6+3}{-1} = \frac{-3}{-1} = 3$$

$$m_2 = \frac{3-1}{-2-4} = \frac{2}{-6} = -\frac{1}{3}$$

The slopes are negative reciprocals, so the lines are perpendicular.

Example: One line passes through the points (-2, 4) and (2, 5); another line passes through the points (-1, 0) and (5, 4). Are these lines parallel, perpendicular or neither?

Find the slopes.

$$m = \frac{y_2 - y_1}{x_2 - x_1}$$

$$m_1 = \frac{5-4}{2-(-2)} = \frac{1}{2+2} = \frac{1}{4}$$

$$m_2 = \frac{4-0}{5-(-1)} = \frac{4}{5+1} = \frac{4}{6} = \frac{2}{3}$$

Since the slopes are not the same, the lines are not parallel. Since they are not negative reciprocals, they are not perpendicular, either. Therefore, the answer is "neither."

Skill 15.2   Use inductive and deductive reasoning.

A simple statement represents a simple idea, that can be described as either "true" or "false", but not both. A simple statement is represented by a small letter of the alphabet.

Example: "Today is Monday." This is a simple statement since it can be determine that this statement is either true or false. We can write p = "Today is Monday".

Example: "John, please be quite". This is not considered a simple statement in our study of logic, since we cannot assign a truth value to it.

Simple statements joined together by **connectives** ("and", "or", "not", "if then", and "if and only if") result in compound statements. Note that compound statements can also be formed using "but", "however", or "never the less". A compound statement can be assigned a truth value.

Conditional statements are frequently written in "if-then" form. The "if" clause of the conditional is known as the **hypothesis**, and the "then" clause is called the **conclusion**. In a proof, the hypothesis is the information that is assumed to be true, while the conclusion is what is to be proven true. A conditional is considered to be of the form: **If p, then q** where p is the hypothesis and q is the conclusion.

p → q is read "if p then q".
~ (statement) is read "it is not true that (statement)".

Quantifiers are words describing a quantity under discussion. These include words like "all', "none" (or "no"), and "some".

Negation of a Statement- If a statement is true, then its negation must be false (and vice versa).

A Summary of Negation Rules:

statement	negation
(1) q	(1) <u>not</u> q
(2) <u>not</u> q	(2) q
(3) π <u>and</u> s	(3) (not π) <u>or</u> (not s)
(4) π <u>or</u> s	(4) (not π) <u>and</u> (not s)
(5) if p, then q	(5) (p) <u>and</u> (not q)

Example: Select the statement that is the negation of "some winter nights are not cold".

A. All winter nights are not cold.
B. Some winter nights are cold.
C. All winter nights are cold.
D. None of the winter nights are cold.

Negation of "some are" is "none are". So the negation statement is "none of the winter night is cold". So the answer is D.

Example: Select the statement that is the negation of "if it rains, then the beach party will not be held".

A. If it does not rain, then the beach party will be held.
B. If the beach party is held, then it will not rain.
C. It does not rain and the beach party will be held.
D. It rains and the beach party will be held.

Negation of "if p, then q" is "p and (not q)". So the negation of the given statement is "it rains and the beach party will be held". So select D.

Example: Select the negation of the statement "If they get elected, then all politicians go back on election promises".

A. If they get elected, then many politicians go back on election promises.
B. They get elected and some politicians go back on election promises.
C. If they do not get elected, some politicians do not go back on election promises.
D. None of the above statements is the negation of the given statement.

Identify the key words of "if...then" and "all...go back". The negation of the given statement is "they get elected and none of the politicians go back on election promises". So select response D, since A, B, and C, statements are not the negations.

Example: Select the statement that is the negation of "the sun is shining bright and I feel great".

A. If the sun is not shining bright. I do not feel great.
B. The sun is not shining bright and I do not feel great.
C. The sun is not shining bring or I do not feel great.
D. the sun is shining bright and I do not feel great.

The negation of "r and s" is "(not r) or (not s)". So the negation of the given statement is "the sun is <u>not</u> shining bright <u>or</u> I do not feel great". We select response C.

Conditional statements can be diagrammed using a **Venn diagram**. A diagram can be drawn with one circle inside another circle. The inner circle represents the hypothesis. The outer circle represents the conclusion. If the hypothesis is taken to be true, then you are located inside the inner circle. If you are located in the inner circle then you are also inside the outer circle, so that proves the conclusion is true.

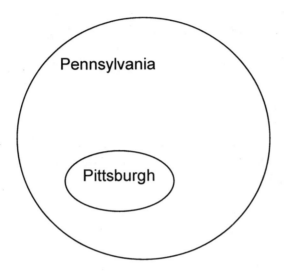

Example: If an angle has a measure of 90 degrees, then it is a right angle.

In this statement "an angle has a measure of 90 degrees" is the hypothesis. In this statement "it is a right angle" is the conclusion.

Example: If you are in Pittsburgh, then you are in Pennsylvania.

In this statement "you are in Pittsburgh" is the hypothesis.
In this statement "you are in Pennsylvania" is the conclusion.

Deductive reasoning is the process of arriving at a conclusion based on other statements that are all known to be true.

A symbolic argument consists of a set of premises and a conclusion in the format of of if [Premise 1 and premise 2] then [conclusion].

An argument is **valid** when the conclusion follows necessarily from the premises. An argument is **invalid** or a fallacy when the conclusion does not follow from the premises.

There are 4 standard forms of valid arguments which must be remembered.

1. Law of Detachment	If p, then q p, Therefore, q	(premise 1) (premise 2)
2. Law of Contraposition	If p, then q not q, Therefore not p	
3. Law of Syllogism	If p, then q If q, then r Therefore if p, then r	
4. Disjunctive Syllogism	p or q not p Therefore, q	

Example: Can a conclusion be reached from these two statements?

A.   All swimmers are athletes.
      All athletes are scholars.

In "if-then" form, these would be:
      If you are a swimmer, then you are an athlete.
      If you are an athlete, then you are a scholar.

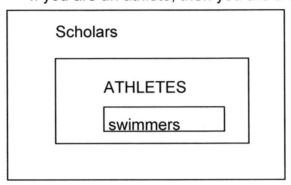

Clearly, if you are a swimmer, then you are also an athlete. This includes you in the group of scholars.

B.   All swimmers are athletes.
      All wrestlers are athletes.

In "if-then" form, these would be:
      If you are a swimmer, then you are an athlete.
      If you are a wrestler, then you are an athlete.

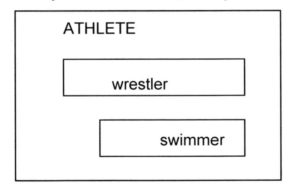

Clearly, if you are a swimmer or a wrestler, then you are also an athlete. This does NOT allow you to come to any other conclusions.

A swimmer may or may NOT also be a wrestler. Therefore, NO CONCLUSION IS POSSIBLE.

Suppose that these statements were given to you, and you are asked to try to reach a conclusion. The statements are:

Example: Determine whether statement A, B, C, or D can be deduced from the following:

(i)If John drives the big truck, then the shipment will be delivered.

(ii)The shipment will not be delivered.

a.John does not drive the big truck.
b.John drives the big truck.
c.The shipment will not be delivered.
d.None of the above conclusion is true.

Let p: John drives the big truck.
    q: The shipment is delivered.

statement (i) gives $p \rightarrow q$, statement (ii) gives $\sim q$. This is the Law of Contraposition.

Therefore, the logical conclusion is $\sim p$ or "John does not drive the big truck". So the answer is response A.

Example: Given that:
(i)Peter is a Jet Pilot or Peter is a Navigator.
(ii)Peter is not a Jet Pilot

Determine which conclusion can be logically deduced.

a.Peter is not a Navigator.
b.Peter is a Navigator.
c.Peter is neither a Jet Pilot nor a Navigator.
d.None of the above is true.

Let p: Peter is a Jet Pilot
    q: Peter is a Navigator.

So we have $p \vee q$ from statement (i)
           $\sim p$ from statement (ii)

So choose response B.

Sample Test: Mathematics

1. $\left(\dfrac{^-4}{9}\right) + \left(\dfrac{^-7}{10}\right) =$

    A. $\dfrac{23}{90}$

    B. $\dfrac{^-23}{90}$

    C. $\dfrac{103}{90}$

    D. $\dfrac{^-103}{90}$

2. $(5.6) \times \left(^-0.11\right) =$

    A. $^-0.616$

    B. 0.616

    C. $^-6.110$

    D. 6.110

3. $(3 \times 9)^4 =$

    A. $(3 \times 9)(3 \times 9)(27 \times 27)$

    B. $(3 \times 9) + (3 \times 9)$

    C. (12×36)

    D. $(3 \times 9) + (3 \times 9) + (3 \times 9)$
        $+ (3 \times 9)$

4. $4\dfrac{2}{9} \times \dfrac{7}{10}$

    A. $4\dfrac{9}{10}$

    B. $\dfrac{266}{90}$

    C. $2\dfrac{43}{45}$

    D. $2\dfrac{6}{20}$

5. $0.74 =$

    A. $\dfrac{74}{100}$

    B. 7.4%

    C. $\dfrac{33}{50}$

    D. $\dfrac{74}{10}$

6. $^-9\dfrac{1}{4}$ $\square$ $^-8\dfrac{2}{3}$

    A. $=$

    B. $<$

    C. $>$

    D. $\leq$

7. 303 is what percent of 600?

    A. 0.505%

    B. 5.05%

    C. 505%

    D. 50.5%

8. A car gets 25.36 miles per gallon. The car has been driven 83,310 miles. What is a reasonable estimate for the number of gallons of gas used?

    A. 2,087 gallons

    B. 3,000 gallons

    C. 1,800 gallons

    D. 164 gallons

9. The owner of a rectangular piece of land 40 yards in length and 30 yards in width wants to divide it into two parts. She plans to join two opposite corners with a fence as shown in the diagram below. The cost of the fence will be approximately $25 per linear foot. What is the estimated cost for the fence needed by the owner?

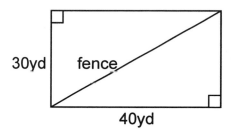

30yd   fence   40yd

    A. $1,250

    B. $62,500

    C. $5,250

    D. $3,750

10. What measure could be used to report the distance traveled in walking around a track?

    A. degrees

    B. square meters

    C. kilometers

    D. cubic feet

11. What is the area of a square whose side is 13 feet?

   A.   169 feet

   B.   169 square feet

   C.   52 feet

   D.   52 square feet

12. The trunk of a tree has a 2.1 meter radius. What is its circumference?

   A. 2.1π square meters

   B. 4.2π meters

   C. 2.1π meters

   D. 4.2π square meters

13. The figure below shows a running track with the shape of a rectangle with semicircles at each end.

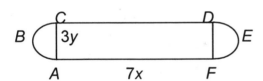

   Calculate the distance around the track.

   A. $6\pi y + 14x$

   B. $3\pi y + 7x$

   C. $6\pi y + 7x$

   D. $3\pi y + 14x$

14. What is the greatest common factor of 16, 28, and 36?

   A.   2

   B.   4

   C.   8

   D.   16

15. Given $f(x) = (x)^3 - 3(x)^2 + 5$, find $x = (-2)$.

   A.   15

   B.   -15

   C.   25

   D.   -25

16. What type of triangle is $\triangle ABC$?

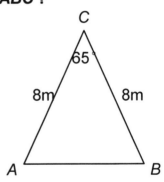

   A.   right

   B.   equilateral

   C.   scalene

   D.   isosceles

17. **Study figures A, B, C, and D. Select the letter in which all triangles are similar.**

A.

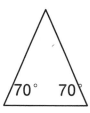

B.

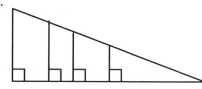

C.

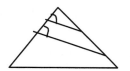

D.

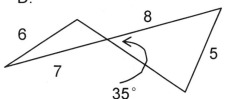

18. **Choose the expression that is not equivalent to 5x + 3y + 15z:**

    A.   5(x + 3z) + 3y

    B.   3(x + y + 5z)

    C.   3y + 5(x + 3z)

    D.   5x + 3(y + 5z)

19. **Choose the statement that is true for all real numbers.**

    A. $a = 0, b \neq 0$, then $\dfrac{b}{a}$ = undefined.

    B. $^-(a + (^-a)) = 2a$

    C. $2(ab) = ^-(2a)b$

    D. $^-a(b + 1) = ab - a$

20. **Choose the equation that is equivalent to the following:**

    $$\frac{3x}{5} - 5 = 5x$$

    A. $3x - 25 = 25x$

    B. $x - \dfrac{25}{3} = 25x$

    C. $6x - 50 = 75x$

    D. $x + 25 = 25x$

21. **If $4x - (3 - x) = 7(x - 3) + 10$, then**

    A. $x = 8$

    B. $x = -8$

    C. $x = 4$

    D. $x = -4$

22. The price of gas was $3.27 per gallon. Your tank holds 15 gallons of fuel. You are using two tanks a week. How much will you save weekly if the price of gas goes down to $2.30 per gallon

   A. $26.00

   B. $29.00

   C. $15.00

   D. $17.00

23. What is the area of this triangle?

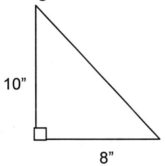

   A.   80 square inches

   B.   20 square inches

   C.   40 square inches

   D.   30 square inches

24. What unit of measurement would describe the spread of a forest fire in a unit time?

   A.   10 square yards per second

   B.   10 yards per minute

   C.   10 feet per hour

   D.   10 cubit feet per hour

25. It takes 5 equally skilled people 9 hours to shingle Mr. Joe's roof. Let *t* be the time required for only 3 of these men to do the same job. Select the correct statement of the given condition.

   A. $\dfrac{3}{5} = \dfrac{9}{t}$

   B. $\dfrac{9}{5} = \dfrac{3}{t}$

   C. $\dfrac{5}{9} = \dfrac{3}{t}$

   D. $\dfrac{14}{9} = \dfrac{t}{5}$

26. In a sample of 40 full-time employees at a particular company, 35 were also holding down a part-time job requiring at least 10 hours/week. If this proportion holds for the entire company of 25000 employees, how many full-time employees at this company are actually holding down a part-time job of at least 10 hours per week.

   A.   714

   B.   625

   C.   21,875

   D.   28,571

27. A student organization is interested in determining how strong the support is among registered voters in the United States for the president's education plan. Which of the following procedures would be most appropriate for selecting a statistically unbiased sample?

   A.   Having viewers call in to a nationally broad-cast talk show and give their opinions.

   B.   Survey registered voters selected by blind drawing in the three largest states.

   C.   Select regions of the country by blind drawing and then select people from the voters registration list by blind drawing.

   D.   Pass out survey forms at the front entrance of schools selected by blind drawing and ask people entering and exiting to fill them in.

28. The following chart shows the yearly average number of international tourists visiting Palm Beach for 1990-1994. How may more international tourists visited Palm Beach in 1994 than in 1991?

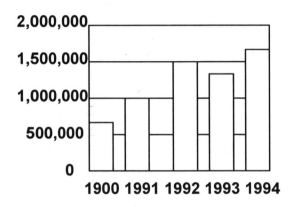

A.   100,000

B.   600,000

C.   1,600,000

D.   8,000,000

29. What is the mode of the data in the following sample?

9, 10, 11, 9, 10, 11, 9, 13

A.   9

B.   9.5

C.   10

D.   11

30. Mary did comparison shopping on her favorite brand of coffee. Over half of the stores priced the coffee at $1.70. Most of the remaining stores priced the coffee at $1.80, except for a few who charged $1.90. Which of the following statements is true about the distribution of prices?

A.   The mean and the mode are the same.
B.   The mean is greater than the mode.
C.   The mean is less than the mode.
D.   The mean is less than the median.

31. Consider the graph of the distribution of the length of time it took individuals to complete an employment form.

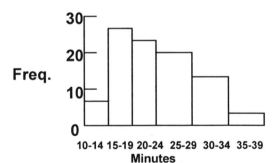

Approximately how many individuals took less than 15 minutes to complete the employment form?

A.   35
B.   28
C.   7
D.   4

32. **Solve for x.**

$$3x - \frac{2}{3} = \frac{5x}{2} + 2$$

  A. $5\frac{1}{3}$

  B. $\frac{17}{3}$

  C.   2

  D. $\frac{16}{2}$

33. **For the following statements**

  I.   **All parallelograms are rectangles**
  II.   **Some rhombuses are squares**
  III.   **All parallelograms are rectangles**

  A.   All statements are correct

  B.   All statements are incorrect

  C.   Only II and III are correct

  D.   Only II is correct

34. $\dfrac{2^{10}}{2^5} =$

  A. 2^2

  B. 2^5

  C. 2^{50}

  D. $2^{\frac{1}{2}}$

35. **What is the equation that expresses the relationship between x and y in the table below?**

x	y
-2	4
-1	2
0	-2
1	-5
2	-8

  A. $y = -x - 2$

  B. $y = -3x - 2$

  C. $y = 3x - 2$

  D. $y = \frac{1}{3}x - 1$

36. Set A, B, C, and U are related as shown in the diagram.

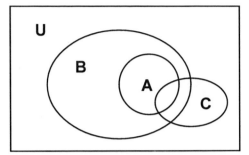

Which of the following is true, assuming not one of the six regions is empty?

A. Any element that is a member of set B is also a member of set A.

B. No element is a member of all three sets A, B, and C.

C. Any element that is a member of set U is also a member of set B.

D. None of the above statements is true.

37. Given that:
i. No athletes are weak.
ii. All football players are athletes.

Determine which conclusion can be logically deduced.

A. Some football players are weak.

B. All football players are weak.

C. No football player is weak.

D. None of the above is true.

38. **All of the following arguments have true conclusions, but one of the arguments is not valid. Select the argument that is not valid.**

   A. All sea stars are echinoderms and all echinoderms are marine; therefore all sea stars are marine.

   B. All spiders are dangerous. The black widow is dangerous. Therefore, the black widow is a spider.

   C. All crocodiles are amphibians and all amphibians breathe by

       lungs, gill, or skin; therefore, all crocodiles breathe by lungs, gill, or skin.

   D. All kids have hats and all boys are kids; therefore, all boys have hats.

39. **Study the information given below. If a logical conclusion is given, select that conclusion.**

   Bob eats donuts or he eats yogurt. If Bob eats yogurt, then he is healthy. If Bob is healthy, then he can run the marathon. Bob does not eat yogurt.

   A. Bob does not eat donuts.

   B. Bob is healthy.

   C. If Bob runs the marathon then he eats yogurt.

   D. None of the above is warranted.

40. **A sofa sells for $520. If the retailer makes a 30% profit, what was the wholesale price?**

   A. $400

   B. $676

   C. $490

   D. $364

41. **Corporate salaries are listed for several employees. Which would be the best measure of central tendency?**

    $24,000 $24,000 $26,000
    $28,000 $30,000 $120,000

    A. Mean

    B. median

    C. mode

    D. no difference

42. **Which statement is true about George's budget?**

    A. George spends the greatest portion of his income on food.

    B. George spends twice as much on utilities as he does on his mortgage.
    C. George spends twice as much on utilities as he does on food.
    D. George spends the same amount on food and utilities as he does on mortgage.

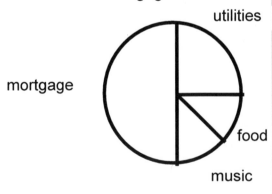

Answer Key: Mathematics

1.	D		22.	B
2.	A		23.	C
3.	A		24.	A
4.	C		25.	B
5.	A		26.	C
6.	B		27.	C
7.	D		28.	B
8.	B		29.	A
9.	D		30.	B
10.	C		31.	C
11.	B		32.	A
12.	B		33.	D
13.	D		34.	A
14.	B		35.	B
15.	B		36.	D
16.	D		37.	C
17.	B		38.	B
18.	B		39.	D
19.	A		40.	A
20.	A		41.	B
21.	C		42.	C

Answers with Rationale

1. Find the LCD of $\dfrac{^-4}{9}$ and $\dfrac{^-7}{10}$. The LCD is 90, so you get

   $\dfrac{^-40}{90} + \dfrac{^-63}{90} = \dfrac{^-103}{90}$, which is answer **D**.

2. Simple multiplication. The answer will be negative because a positive times a negative is a negative number. $5.6 \times ^-0.11 = ^-0.616$, which is answer **A**.

3. $(3 \times 9)^4 = (3 \times 9)(3 \times 9)(3 \times 9)(3 \times 9)$, which, when solving two of the parentheses, is $(3 \times 9)(3 \times 9)(27 \times 27)$, which is answer **A**.

4. Convert any mixed number to an improper fraction: $\dfrac{38}{9} \, x \, \dfrac{7}{10}$. Since no common factors of numerators or denominators exist, multiply the numerators and the denominators by each other $= \dfrac{266}{90}$. Convert back to a mixed number and reduce $2\dfrac{86}{90} = 2\dfrac{43}{45}$. The answer is **C**.

5. $0.74 \rightarrow$ the 4 is in the hundredths place, so the answer is $\dfrac{74}{100}$, which is **A**.

6. The larger the absolute value of a negative number, the smaller the negative number is. The absolute value of $-9\dfrac{1}{4}$ is $9\dfrac{1}{4}$ which is larger than the absolute value of $-8\dfrac{2}{3}$ is $8\dfrac{2}{3}$. Therefore, the sign should be $-9\dfrac{1}{4} < -8\dfrac{2}{3}$, which is answer **B**.

7. Use x for the percent. $600x = 303$. $\dfrac{600x}{600} = \dfrac{303}{600} \rightarrow x = 0.505 = 50.5\%$, which is answer **D**.

8. Divide the number of miles by the miles per gallon to determine the approximate number of gallons of gas used. $\dfrac{83310 \text{ miles}}{25.36 \text{ miles per gallon}} = 3285$ gallons. This is approximately 3000 gallons, which is answer **B**.

9. Find the length of the diagonal by using the Pythagorean theorem. Let x be the length of the diagonal.

$$30^2 + 40^2 = x^2 \to 900 + 1600 = x^2$$
$$2500 = x^2 \to \sqrt{2500} = \sqrt{x^2}$$
$$x = 50 \text{ yards}$$

Convert to feet. $\dfrac{50 \text{ yards}}{x \text{ feet}} = \dfrac{1 \text{ yard}}{3 \text{ feet}} \to 1500 \text{ feet}$

It cost $25.00 per linear foot, so the cost is (1500 ft)($25) = $3750, which is answer **D**.

10. Degrees measures angles, square meters measures area, cubic feet measure volume, and kilometers measures length. Kilometers is the only reasonable answer, which is **C**.

11. Area = length times width (*lw*).
Length = 13 feet
Width = 13 feet (square, so length and width are the same).
Area = $13 \times 13 = 169$ square feet.
Area is measured in square feet. So the answer is **B**.

12. Circumference is $2\pi r$, where r is the radius. The circumference is $2\pi 2.1 = 4.2\pi$ meters (not square meters because not measuring area), which is answer **B**.

13. The two semicircles of the track create one circle with a diameter 3y. The circumference of a circle is $C = \pi d$ so $C = 3\pi y$. The length of both sides of the track is 7x each side, so the total circumference around the track is $3\pi y + 7x + 7x = 3\pi y + 14x$,
which is answer **D**.

14. The smallest number in this set is 16; its factors are 1, 2, 4, 8 and 16. 16 in the largest factor, but it does not divide into 28 or 36. Neither does 8. 4 does factor into both 28 and 36. The answer is **B**.

15. Substitute $x = -2$.

$$f(-2) = (^-2)^3 - 3 \times (^-2)^2 + 5$$
$$f(-2) = ^- 8 - 3(4) + 5$$
$$f(-2) = ^- 8 - 12 + 5$$
$$f(-2) = ^- 15$$

The answer is **B**.

16. Two of the sides are the same length, so we know the triangle is either equilateral or isosceles. $\angle CAB$ and $\angle CBA$ are equal, because their sides are. Therefore, $180° = 65° - 2x = \dfrac{115°}{2} = 57.5°$. Because all three angles are not equal, the triangle is isosceles, so the answer is **D**.

17. Choice A is not correct because one triangle is equilateral and the other is isosceles. Choice C is not correct because the two smaller triangles are similar, but the large triangle is not. Choice D is not correct because the lengths and angles are not proportional to each other. Therefore, the correct answer is **B** because all the triangles have the same angles.

18. $5x + 3y + 15z = (5x + 15z) + 3y = 5(x + 3z) + 3y$ A. is true
    $= 5x + (3y + 15z) = 5x + 3(y + 5z)$ D. is true
    $= 37 + (5x + 15z) = 37 + 5(x + 3z)$ C is true

    These can all be solved using the associative property and then factoring. However, in B. $3(x + y + 5z)$ by distributive property $= 3x + 3y + 15z$ does not equal $5x + 37 + 15z$. The answer is **B**.

19. **A** is the correct answer because any number divided by 0 is undefined.

20. **A** is the correct answer because it is the original equation multiplied by 5. The other choices alter the answer to the original equation.

21. Solve for x.

    $4x - (3 - x) = 7(x - 3) + 10$

    $4x - 3 + x = 7x - 21 + 10$

    $5x - 3 = 7x - 11$

    $5x = 7x - 11 + 3$ The answer is **C**.

    $5x - 7x = {}^{-}8$

    ${}^{-}2x = {}^{-}8$

    $x = 4$

22. 15 gallons x 2 tanks = 30 gallons a week
    = 30 gallons x $3.27 = $98.10
    30 gallons x $2.30 = $69.00
    $98.10 - $69.00 = $29.10 is approximately $29.00. The answer is **B**.

23. The area of a triangle is $\frac{1}{2}bh$.

    $\frac{1}{2}x8x10 = 40$ square inches. The answer is **C**.

24. The only appropriate answer is one that describes "an area" of forest consumed per unit time. All answers are not units of area measurement except answer **A**.

25. $\dfrac{9 \text{ hours}}{5 \text{ people}} = \dfrac{3 \text{ people}}{t \text{ hours}}$ The answer is **B**.

26. $\dfrac{35}{40}$ full time employees have a part time job also. Out of 25,000 full time employees, the number that have a part time job also is

    $\dfrac{35}{40} = \dfrac{x}{25000} \rightarrow 40x = 875000 \rightarrow x = 21875$, so 21875 full time employees also have a part time job. The answer is **C**.

27. **C** would be the best answer because it is random and it surveys a larger population.

28. The number of tourists in 1991 was 1,000,000 and the number in 1994 was 1,600,000. Subtract to get a difference of 600,000, which is answer **B.**

29. The mode is the number that appears most frequently. 9 appears 3 times, which is more than the other numbers. Therefore the answer is **A.**

30. Over half the stores priced the coffee at $1.70, so this means that this is the mode. The mean would be slightly over $1.70 because other stores priced the coffee at over $1.70. Therefore, the answer is **B.**

31. According to the chart, the number of people who took under 15 minutes is 7, which is answer **C.**

32. $3x(6) - \dfrac{2}{3}(6) = \dfrac{5x}{2}(6) + 2(6)$ 6 is the LCD of 2 and 3

$18x - 4 = 15x + 12$

$18x = 15x + 16$

$3x = 16$

$x = \dfrac{16}{3} = 5\dfrac{1}{3}$ which is answer **A.**

33. I is false because only some parallelograms are rectangles. II true. III is false because only some parallelograms are rhombuses. So only II is correct, which is answer **D.**

34. The quotient rule of exponents says $\dfrac{a^m}{a^n} = a^{(m-n)}$ so $\dfrac{2^{10}}{2^5} = 2^{(10-5)} = 2^5$

which is answer **B.**

35. Solve by plugging in the values of x and y into the equations to see if they work. The answer is **B.** because it is the only equation for which the values of x and y are correct.

36. Answer A is incorrect because not all members of set B are also in set A. Answer B is incorrect because there are elements that are members of all three sets A, B, and C. Answer C is incorrect because not all members of set U is a member of set B. This leaves answer **D**, which states that none of the above choices are true.

37. **C**

38. **B**

39. **D**

40. $400; Let x be the wholesale price, then x + .30x = 520, 1.30x = 520. divide both sides by 1.30. **A**

41. The median provides the best measure of central tendency in this case where the mode is the lowest number and the mean would be disproportionately skewed by the outlier $120,000. **B**

42. George spends twice as much on utilities as he does on food; George spends twice as much on utilities as on food. **C.**

DOMAIN III.   WRITING

The candidate may be asked to respond to persuasive and/or expository writing exercises in which the candidate is asked to do one or more of the following:

- Compose a fluent, focused, and sustained piece of writing on a given topic using language and style appropriate to a specified audience, purpose, and occasion
- State and maintain a clear main idea and point of view using effective organization to enhance meaning and clarity
- Take a position on a contemporary social or political issue and defend that position with reasoned arguments and supporting examples
- Use effective sentence structure
- Demonstrate the ability to spell, capitalize, and punctuate according to standard writing conventions

Responses to the writing assignment will be evaluated according to the following performance characteristics:

- Focus and Appropriateness – The fluency and quality of the discussion, and the sustained attention on a given topic using language and style appropriate to a specified audience, purpose, and occasion
- Unity and Organization – The effectiveness of the organization, the logical sequence of ideas, and the clarity of the writing used to state and maintain a main idea and point of view
- Development and Rationale – The relevance, depth, and effectiveness of statements or arguments and examples used to support those statements or defend a position
- Usage and Sentence Structure – The precision in word choice and use of effective sentence structure
- Mechanical Conventions – The use of spelling, capitalization, and punctuation according to standard writing conventions

ESSAY GUIDELINES

Even before you select a topic, determine what each prompt is asking you to discuss. This first decision is crucial. If you pick a topic you don't really understand or about which you have little to say, you'll have difficulty developing your essay. So take a few moments to analyze each topic carefully *before* you begin to write.

Topic A: A modern invention that can be considered a wonder of the world

In general, the topic prompts have two parts:
    the *SUBJECT* of the topic and
    an *ASSERTION* about the subject.

The **subject** is *a modern invention*. In this prompt, the word *modern* indicates you should discuss something invented recently, at least in this century. The word *invention* indicated you're to write about something created by humans (not natural phenomena such as mountains or volcanoes). You may discuss an invention that has potential for harm, such as chemical warfare or the atomic bomb; or you may discuss an invention that has the potential for good: the computer, DNA testing, television, antibiotics, and so on.

The **assertion** (a statement of point of view) is that *the invention has such powerful or amazing qualities that it should be considered a wonder of the world.* The assertion states your point of view about the subject, and it limits the range for discussion. In other words, you would discuss particular qualities or uses of the invention, not just discuss how it was invented or whether it should have been invented at all.

Note also that this particular topic encourages you to use examples to show the reader that a particular invention is a modern wonder. Some topic prompts lend themselves to essays with an argumentative edge, one in which you take a stand on a particular issue and persuasively prove your point. Here, you undoubtedly could offer examples or illustrations of the many "wonders" and uses of the particular invention you chose.

Be aware that misreading or misinterpreting the topic prompt can lead to serious problems. Papers that do not address the topic occur when one reads too quickly or only half-understands the topic. This may happen if you misread or misinterpret words. Misreading can also lead to a paper that addresses only part of the topic prompt rather than the entire topic.

To develop a complete essay, spend a few minutes planning. Jot down your ideas and quickly sketch an outline. Although you may feel under pressure to begin writing, you will write more effectively if you plan out your major points.

Prewriting

Before actually writing, you'll need to generate content and to develop a writing plan. Three prewriting techniques that can be helpful are:

Brainstorming

When brainstorming, quickly create a list of words and ideas that are connected to the topic. Let your mind roam free to generate as many relevant ideas as possible in a few minutes. For example, on the topic of computers you may write

computer- modern invention
types- personal computers, micro-chips in calculators and watches
wonder - acts like an electronic brain
uses - science, medicine, offices, homes, schools
problems- too much reliance; the machines aren't perfect

This list could help you focus on the topic and states the points you could develop in the body paragraphs. The brainstorming list keeps you on track and is well worth the few minutes it takes to jot down the ideas. While you haven't ordered the ideas, seeing them on paper is an important step.

Questioning

Questioning helps you focus as you mentally ask a series of exploratory questions about the topic. You may use the most basic questions: **who, what, where, when, why, and how.**

"What is my subject? "
    [computers]

"What types of computers are there?"
    [personal computers, micro-chip computers]

"Why have computers been a positive invention?"
    [acts like an electronic brain in machinery and equipment; helps solve complex scientific problems]

"How have computers been a positive invention?"
    [used to make improvements in:
- science (space exploration, moon landings)
- mehcine (MRIs, CAT scans, surgical tools, research models)
- business (PCs, FAX, telephone equipment)
- education (computer programs for math, languages, science, social studies), and
- personal use (family budgets, **tax** programs, healthy diet plans)]

"How can I show that computers are good?"
    [citing numerous examples]

"What problems do I see with computers?"
    [too much reliance; not yet perfect.]

"What personal experiences would help me develop examples to respond to this topic?
    [my own experiences using computers]

Of course, you may not have time to write out the questions completely. You might just write the words *who, what, where, why, how* and the major points next to each. An abbreviated list might look as follows:

What — computers/modern wonder/making life better
How — through technological improvements: lasers, calculators, CAT scans, MUs.

Where – in science and space exploration, medicine, schools, offices

In a few moments, your questions should help you to focus on the topic and to generate interesting ideas and points to make in the essay. Later in the writing process, you can look back at the list to be sure you've made the key points you intended.

Clustering

Some visual thinkers find clustering an effective prewriting method. when clustering, you draw a box in the center of your paper and write your topic within that box. Then you draw lines from the center box and connect it to small satellite boxes that contain related ideas. Note the cluster below on computers:

SAMPLE CLUSTER

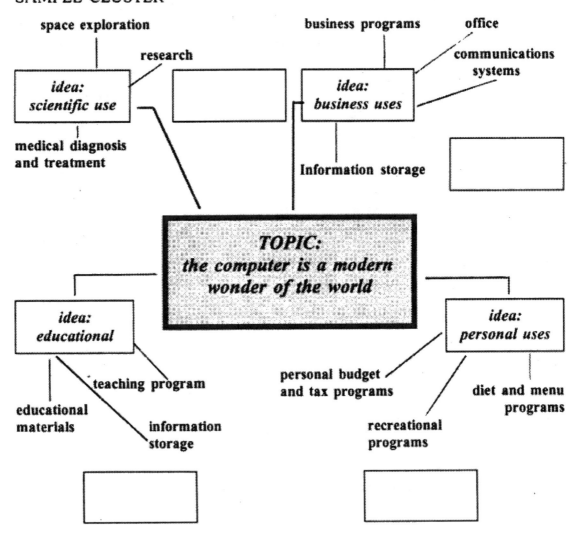

Writing the Thesis

After focusing on the topic and generating your ideas, form your thesis, the controlling idea of your essay. The thesis is your general statement to the reader that expresses your point of view and guides your essay's purpose and scope. The thesis should allow you either to explain your subject or to take an arguable position about it. A strong thesis statement is neither too narrow nor too broad.

Subject and Assertion of the Thesis

From the analysis of the general topic, you saw the topic in terms of its two parts - *subject* and *assertion*. On the exam, your thesis or viewpoint on a particular topic is stated in two important points:

1.   the *SUBJECT* of the paper
2.   the *ASSERTION* about the subject.

The **subject of the thesis** relates directly to the topic prompt but expresses the specific area you have chosen to discuss. (Remember the exam topic will be general and will allow you to choose a particular subject related to the topic). For example, the computer is one modern invention.

The **assertion of the thesis** is your viewpoint, or opinion, about the subject. The assertion provides the motive or purpose for your essay, and it may be an arguable point or one that explains or illustrates a point of view.

For example, you may present an argument for or against a particular issue. You may contrast two people, objects, or methods to show that one is better than the other. You may analyze a situation in all aspects and make recommendations for improvement. You may assert that a law or policy should be adopted, changed or abandoned. You may also, as in the computer example, explain to your reader that a situation or condition exists; rather than argue a viewpoint, you would use examples to illustrate your assertion about the essay's subject.

Specifically, the **subject** of Topic A is *the computer*. The **assertion** is that *it is a modern wonder that has improved our lives and that we rely on*. Now you quickly have created a workable thesis in a few moments:

> *The computer is a modern wonder of the world that has improved our lives and that we have come to rely on.*

Guidelines for Writing Thesis Statements

The following guidelines are not a formula for writing thesis statements but rather are general strategies for making your thesis statement clearer and more effective.

1. State a *particular point* of *view* about the topic with both a *subject* and an *assertion.* The thesis should give the essay purpose and scope and thus provide the reader a guide. If the thesis is vague, your essay may be undeveloped because you do not have an idea to assert or a point to explain. Weak thesis statements are often framed as facts, questions or announcements:

    a. Avoid a fact statement as a thesis. While a fact statement may provide a subject, it generally does not include a point of view about the subject that provides the basis for an extended discussion. Example: *Recycling saved our community over $10,000 last year.* This fact statement provides a detail, *not* a point of view. Such a detail might be found within an essay but it does not state a point of view.

    b. Avoid framing the thesis as a vague question. In many cases, rhetorical questions do not provide a clear point of view for an extended essay. Example: *How do people recycle?* This question neither asserts a point of view nor helpfully guides the reader to understand the essay's purpose and scope.

    c. Avoid the "announcer" topic sentence that merely states the topic you will discuss
        Example: *I will discuss ways to recycle.* This sentence states the subject but the scope of the essay is only suggested. Again, this statement does not assert a viewpoint that guides the essay's purpose. It merely "announces" that the writer will write about the topic.

2. Start with a workable thesis. You might revise your thesis as you begin writing and discover your own point of view.

3. If feasible and appropriate, perhaps state the thesis in multi-point form, expressing the scope of the essay. By stating the points in parallel form, you clearly lay out the essay's plan for the reader.
    Example: *To improve the environment, we can recycle our trash, elect politicians who see the environment as a priority, and support lobbying groups who work for environmental protection.*

4. Because of the exam time limit, place your thesis in the first paragraph to key the reader to the essay's main idea.

Creating a working outline

A good thesis gives structure to your essay and helps focus your thoughts. When forming your thesis, look at your prewriting strategy – clustering, questioning, or brainstorming. Then decide quickly which two or three major areas you'll discuss. Remember you must limit *the scope* of the paper because of the time factor.

The **outline** lists those main areas or points as topics for each paragraph. Looking at the prewriting cluster on computers, you might choose several areas in which computers help us, for example in science and medicine, business, and education. You might also consider people's reliance on this "wonder" and include at least one paragraph about this reliance. A formal outline for this essay might look like the one below:

I.   Introduction and thesis
II. Computers used in science and medicine
II. Computers used in business
IV. Computers used in education
V.   People's reliance on computers
VI. Conclusion

Under time pressure, however, you may use a shorter organizational plan, such as abbreviated key words in a list. For example

1. intro: wonders of the computer OR
2. science
3. med
4. schools
5. business
6. conclusion

a. intro: wonders of computers - science
b. in the space industry
c. in medical technology
d. conclusion

Developing the essay

With a working thesis and outline, you can begin writing the essay. The essay should be in three main sections:

1) The **introduction** sets up the essay and leads to the thesis statement.
2) The **body paragraphs** are developed with concrete information leading from the **topic sentences**.
3) The **conclusion** ties the essay together.

Introduction

Put your thesis statement into a clear, coherent opening paragraph. One effective device is to use a funnel approach in which you begin with a brief description of the broader issue and then move to a clearly focused, specific thesis statement.

Consider the following introductions to the essay on computers. The length of each is an obvious difference. Read each and consider the other differences.

Does each introduce the subject generally?
Does each lead to a stated thesis?
Does each relate to the topic prompt?

Introduction 1: *Computers are used every day. They have many uses. Some people who use them are workers, teachers and doctors.*

Analysis: This introduction does give the general topic, computers used every day, but it does not explain what those uses are. This introduction does not offer a point of view in a clearly stated thesis nor does it convey the idea that computers are a modem wonder.

Introduction 2: *Computers are used just about everywhere these days. I don't think there's an office around that doesn't use computers, and we use them a lot in all kinds of jobs. Computers are great for making life easier and work better. I don't think we'd get along without the computer.*

Analysis: This introduction gives the general topic about computers and mentions one area that uses computers. The thesis states that people couldn't get along without computers, but it does not state the specific areas the essay discusses. Note, too, the meaning is not helped by vague diction such as *a lot* or *great.*

Introduction 3: *Each day we either use computers or see them being used around us. We wake to the sound of a digital alarm operated by a micro-chip. Our cars run by computerized machinery. We use computers to help us learn. We receive phone calls and letters transferred from computers across continents. Our astronauts walked on the moon, and returned safely, all because of computer technology. The computer a wonderful electronic brain that we have come to rely on, and has changed our world through advances in science, business, and education.*

Analysis: This introduction is the most thorough and fluent because it provides interest in the general topic and offers specific information about computers as a modern wonder. It also leads to a thesis that directs the reader to the scope of the discussion--advances in science, business, and education.

Topic Sentences

Just as the essay must have an overall focus reflected in the thesis statement, each paragraph must have a central idea reflected in the topic sentence. A good topic sentence also provides transition from the previous paragraph and relates to the essay's thesis. Good topic sentences, therefore, provide unity throughout the essay.

Consider the following potential topic sentences. Be sure that each provides transition and clearly states the subject of the paragraph.

Topic Sentence 1: *Computers are used in science.*

Analysis: This sentence simply states the topic--computers used in science. It does not relate to the thesis or provide transition from the introduction. The reader still does not know how computers are used.

Topic Sentence 2: *Now I will talk about computers used in science.*

Analysis: Like the faulty "announcer" thesis statement, this "announcer" topic sentence is vague and merely names the topic.

Topic Sentence 3: *First, computers used in science have improved our lives.*

Analysis: The transition word *First* helps link the introduction and this paragraph. It adds unity to the essay. It does not, however, give specifics about the improvement computers have made in our lives.

Topic Sentence 4: *First used in scientific research and spaceflights, computers are now used extensively in the diagnosis and treatment of disease.*

Analysis: This sentence is the most thorough and fluent. It provides specific areas that will be discussed in the paragraph and offers more than an announcement of the topic. The writer gives concrete information about the content of the paragraph that will follow.

Summary Guidelines for Writing Topic Sentences
1. Specifically relate the topic to the thesis statement.
2. State clearly and concretely the subject of the paragraph
3. Provide some transition from the previous paragraph
4. Avoid topic sentences that are facts, questions, or announcers.

Supporting Details

If you have a good thesis and a good outline, you should be able to construct a complete essay. Your paragraphs should contain concrete, interesting information and supporting details to support your point of view. As often as possible, create images in your reader's mind. Fact statements also add weight to your opinions, especially when you are trying to convince the reader of you viewpoint. Because every good thesis has an assertion, you should offer specifics, facts, data, anecdotes, expert opinion, and other details to *show* or *prove* that assertion. While *you* know what you mean, your *reader* does not. On the exam, you must explain and develop ideas as fully as possible in the time allowed.

In the following paragraph, the sentences in **bold print** provide a skeleton of a paragraph on the benefits of recycling. The sentences in bold are generalizations that by themselves do not explain the need to recycle. The sentences in *italics* add details to SHOW the general points in bold. Notice how the supporting details help you understand the necessity for recycling.

While one day recycling may become mandatory in all states, right now it is voluntary in many communities. *Those of us who participate in recycling are amazed by how much material is recycled.* **For many communities, the blue-box recycling program has had an immediate effect.** *By just recycling glass, aluminum cans, and plastic bottles, we have reduced the volume of disposable trash by one third, thus extending the useful life of local landfills by over a decade. Imagine the difference if those dramatic results were achieved nationwide.* **The amount of reusable items we thoughtlessly dispose of is staggering.** *For example, Americans dispose of enough steel everyday to supply Detroit car manufacturers for three months. Additionally, we dispose of enough aluminum annually to rebuild the nation's airfleet. These statistics, available from the Environmental Protection Agency (EPA), should encourage all of us to watch what we throw away.* **Clearly, recycling in our homes and in our communities directly improves the environment.**

Notice how the author's supporting examples enhance the message of the paragraph and relate to the author's thesis noted above. If you only read the bold-face sentences, you have a glimpse at the topic. This paragraph of, illustration, however, is developed through numerous details creating specific images: *reduced the volume of disposable trash by one-third; extended the useful life of local landfills by over a decade; enough steel everyday to supply Detroit car manufacturers for three months; enough aluminum to rebuild the nation's airfleet.* If the writer had merely written a few general sentences, as those shown in bold face, you would not fully understand the vast amount of trash involved in recycling or the positive results of current recycling efforts.

End your essay with a brief straightforward **concluding paragraph** that ties together the essay's content and leaves the reader with a sense of its completion. The conclusion should: reinforce the main points and offer some insight into the topic, provide a sense of unity for the essay by relating it to the thesis and signal clear closure of the essay.

On the next page is sample strong response to the prompt:
A problem people recognize and should do something about

Sample Strong Response

Does the introduction help orient the reader to the topic?

Is there a thesis? Does it clearly state the main idea of the essay?

Does each paragraph have a topic sentence that provides transition and defines the idea?

Do the paragraphs purposefully support the thesis? Do they have interesting details and examples?

Time magazine, which typically selects a person of the year, chose Earth as the planet of the year in 1988 to underscore the severe problems facing our planet and therefore us. We hear dismal reports everyday about the water shortage, the ozone depletion, and the obscene volume of trash generated by our society. Because the problem is global, many people feel powerless to help. Fortunately, by being environmentally aware, we can take steps to alter what seems inevitable. we can recycle our trash and support politicians and lobbying groups who will work for laws to protect the environment.

While one day recycling may be mandatory in all states, right now it is voluntary in many communities. Those of us who participate in recycling are amazed by how much material is recycled. For many communities, the blue box recycling program has had an immediate effect. by just recycling glass, aluminum cans, and plastic bottles, we have reduced the volume of disposable trash by one-third, thus extending the useful life of local landfills by over a decade. Imagine the difference if those dramatic results were achieved nationwide. The amount of reusable items we thoughtlessly dispose of is staggering. For example, Americans dispose of enough steep everyday to supply Detroit car manufacturers for three months. Additionally, we dispose of enough aluminum annually to rebuild the nation's air fleet. These statistics, available from the Environmental Protection Agency (EPA) should encourage us to watch what we throw away. Clearly, recycling in our homes and communities directly improves the environment.

Are the paragraphs unified and coherent? Is the material in each paragraph relevant and important?

Moreover, we must be aware of the political issues involved in environmental protection because, unfortunately, the environmental crisis continues despite policies and laws on the books. Enacted in the 1970s, the federal Clean Water Act was intended to clean up polluted waters through the nation and to provide safe drinking water for everyone. However, today, with the Water Act still in place, dangerous medical waste has washed onto public beaches in Florida and recently several people died from the polluted drinking water in Madison Wisconsin. Additionally, contradictory government policies often work against resource protection. For example, some state welfare agencies give new mothers money only for disposable, not cloth, diapers. In fact, consumer groups found that cloth diapers are cheaper initially and save money over time as we struggle with the crisis of bulging landfills. Clearly, we need consistent government policies and stiffer laws to ensure mandatory enforcement and heavy fines for polluters. We can do this best by electing politicians who will fight for such laws and voting out those who won't.

Does the conclusion tie the essay together?

Is the essay edited for grammar and mechanical errors?

We can also work to save our planet by supporting organizations that lobby for meaningful, enforceable legal changes. Most of us do not have time to write letters, send telegrams, or study every issue concerning the environment. We can join several organizations that act as watchdogs for us all. For example, organizations such as Greenpeace, the Cousteau Society and the Sierra Club all offer memberships for as low as 15 dollars. By supporting these organizations, we ensure that they have the necessary resources to keep working for all of us and do not have to alter their standards because they must accept funding from special interest groups.

Clearly, we all must become environmentally aware. Only through increase awareness can we avoid the tragic consequences of living on a dying planet. We must actively support recycling programs and support those who fight to protect our fragile environment.

Analysis: While not every essay needs to be this thorough in order to pass the exam, this essay shows that with a clear thesis and concept in mind, a writer can produce a literate, interesting piece at one sitting. The introduction creates interest in the general topic and leads to a thesis in the last sentence. The reader has a very clear idea what will be addressed in the essay, and all body paragraphs have topic sentences that relate to the thesis and provide transition. The numerous supporting details and examples are presented in the sophisticated style that reads easily and is enhanced by a college-level vocabulary and word choice. Transition words and phrases add unity to sentences and paragraphs. Grammar and mechanics areas are correct, so errors don't detract from the fine writing. For all these reasons, this essay is a polished piece of writing deserving of an upper-range score.

XAMonline, INC. 21 Orient Ave. Melrose, MA 02176

Toll Free number 800-301-4647

TO ORDER Fax 781-662-9268 OR www.XAMonline.com

MICHIGAN TEST FOR TEACHER EXAMINATION - MTTC - 2007

PO#   Store/School:

Address 1:

Address 2 (Ship to other):

City, State Zip

Credit card number_____-_____-_____-_____   expiration_____

EMAIL _____

PHONE   **FAX**

13# ISBN 2007	TITLE	Qty	Retail	Total
978-1-58197-968-8	MTTC Basic Skills 96			
978-1-58197-954-1	MTTC Biology 17			
978-1-58197-955-8	MTTC Chemistry 18			
978-1-58197-957-2	MTTC Earth-Space Science 20			
978-1-58197-966-4	MTTC Elementary Education 83			
978-1-58197-967-1	MTTC Elementary Education 83 Sample Questions			
978-1-58197-950-3	MTTC English 02			
978-1-58197-961-9	MTTC Family and Consumer Sciences 40			
978-1-58197-959-6	MTTC French Sample Test 23			
978-1-58197-965-7	MTTC Guidance Counselor 51			
978-1-58197-964-0	MTTC Humanities& Fine Arts 53, 54			
978-1-58197-969-5	MTTC Integrated Sciences (Secondary) 17			
978-1-58197-953-4	MTTC Learning Disabled 63			
978-1-58197-963-3	MTTC Library Media 48			
978-1-58197-958-9	MTTC Mathematics (Secondary) 22			
978-1-58197-962-6	MTTC Physical Education 44			
978-1-58197-956-5	MTTC Physics Sample Test 19			
978-1-58197-952-7	MTTC Political Science 10			
978-1-58197-951-0	MTTC Reading 05			
978-1-58197-972-5	MTTC Science 16			
978-1-58197-960-2	MTTC Spanish 28			
978-158197-970-1	MTTC Social Studies 84			
			SUBTOTAL	
FOR PRODUCT PRICES GO TO WWW.XAMONLINE.COM			**Ship**	$8.25
			TOTAL	

CPSIA information can be obtained at www.ICGtesting.com
Printed in the USA
BVOW051448040112

279805BV00004B/15/A